D1586683

BORDER COLLIES
A BREED APART

A TRILOGY
CAROL PRICE

Copyright © 2019 by Carol Price and First Stone Publishing

First published in 2019 by First Stone Publishing,
an imprint of Westline Publishing Limited
The Old Hen House, St Martin's Farm, Zeals,
Warminster BA12 6NZ United Kingdom.
ISBN 978 1 910488 54 6

All rights reserved. No part of this book may be used or
reproduced in any manner whatsoever, including electronic
media or photocopying, without written permission from
the publisher, except in the case of brief quotations embodied
in critical reviews.

Cover and interior design: Alan Cooper

Printed in China via Printworks Global

1 2 3 4 5 6 7 8 9 0

This book series is dedicated to
ILONA (Bryanru Ilona)
1998-2015
My dog of a lifetime

And her equally irreplaceable son,
ARUN (Spirit of Ilona)
2003-2018
A dog with a heart of gold

How lucky I have been to have owned, known and loved dogs like you

PHOTOS: ©CAROL PRICE

BOOK THREE

BEHAVIOUR
Insights, Issues and Solutions

CAROL PRICE

CONTENTS

A BREED APART

Understanding and managing breed behaviour

We need to understand both the breed – and the individual – to form meaningful partnerships with our dogs.

Hopefully, the first two books in this *Breed Apart* series will have given you far greater insight into the mental differences that exist between Border Collies and other dogs, why those differences exist, and where they come from in the breed's genetic past.

Book Two, *Essential Life Skills and Learning*, also outlined how an increased understanding of your Collie's inner psychology will help you to train him to best effect, including channelling and controlling his 'working instinct' and greater development and enhancement of his 'social' brain. The latter is critical for dogs within the breed who might otherwise develop more fearful or defensive reactions in many social situations. This is often a result of having poorer social recognition or awareness, as well as a greater aversion to stranger sensory or social experiences. This is typical in dogs with more autistic kinds of minds and thinking patterns.

Now, in the third and last book in this series, we are going to look at all aspects of breed behaviour, as well as how, more specifically, Border Collies may vary from each other as individuals despite belonging to the same breed (see Chapter 2: *The Collie Spectrum*).

I will be exploring the roots of fear and/or aggression in Border Collies, more obsessive-compulsive patterns of behaviour (such as persistent eyeing and chasing), as well as the extent to which behaviour in these dogs stems from the sub-conscious, as opposed to conscious, mind. I will also be looking at why some Collies cope so badly when separated from their owners, and what you can do to lower the mental temperature of a dog experiencing more extreme over-arousal, or sensory overload.

As ever, so much of the way a Collie chooses to think, or react, can be rooted in his more individual kind of mental wiring. But the better we get at understanding this mental wiring, the more successful our management of these dogs should be, and similarly the better placed we should be to address – and hopefully overcome – any number of different behaviour issues in them.

CHAPTER 1:

WHAT IS GOING WRONG WITH YOUR DOG?

Why are some Collies more difficult than others?

Some Collies will always be more challenging to own and, at the heart of this, lies a more sensitive and complex inner psychology.

Much of what goes wrong in a Border Collie can begin with his breeding. Or, more precisely, an inherited disposition for more challenging mental traits which often have an autistic element to them - as outlined in greater detail in Chapter 4: *Knowing your dog's mind.*

People do not always understand the link between a certain kind of genetic brain in a dog, and a subsequent type of personality and behaviour in him. But it is always there. Similarly there are people who may more readily dismiss the notion that dogs can be autistic in their thinking, or behaviour, on the basis that there is no firm scientific proof to confirm it.

As it happens, there is no firm scientific proof to confirm that autism exists in humans, either. It remains a condition most commonly diagnosed through the observation of specific mental and behavioural traits. These traits can vary greatly among individuals in terms of intensity of expression, but they still conform to a consistently recurring pattern. In much the same way do I see consistently recurring patterns of more autistic thinking and behaviour in Border Collies.

Advance warnings

For the newer Collie owner, or owner to be, a key complicating factor, when trying to choose a potentially less challenging future dog, is that more testing mental breed traits aren't always that obvious in younger puppies – unless you have a rather more experienced eye, or a better grasp of what kind of pedigrees typically produce that kind of dog. So instead, these traits will tend to reveal themselves more gradually, as the dog gets older. Earliest warning signs can include a puppy showing a more noticeable level of nervousness or fearfulness, and a greater reluctance to socially engage with others, be they human or canine.

Often, owners will dismiss, or overlook, such behaviour as being commonplace, or even normal, in a young puppy, or something they can easily fix or improve later, with the right amount of love and care. And sometimes they are right, especially with the benefit of optimum rearing and training practices (as outlined in Book Two). But at other times they are sadly proved wrong because the dog's mental troubles or issues just run too deep.

Not everyone will appreciate the link between a certain kind of genetic brain in a dog and specific types of personality and behaviour which, in the Collie, can include more obsessive instincts and impulses.

UNDERSTANDING MORE AUTISTIC PATTERNS OF BEHAVIOUR IN YOUR DOG

As explained throughout this book series, many odd, disturbing, and challenging behaviours seen in Border Collies are easier to understand when seen in the context of these dogs having essentially more autistic minds. This should always be factored in when considering any kind of problem behaviour you may be experiencing with your own dog.

To recap, more autistic patterns of behaviour in Collies include the following:

- Hypersensitivity to visual stimuli – objects and bright lights may also appear to jump around and fragment.
- Over-sensitivity to sensory experiences like noise, touch, smells, crowds and excess movement.
- Difficulties with social communication/ interaction, and a tendency to find most social situations demanding and stressful.
- Inability to read social cues or body language well. Normal or benign social approaches by others may be seen as threatening.

- Greater social disconnection in general, i.e. lack of interest in any form of social engagement with others, or ability to recognise others as fellow 'social beings'.
- A tendency to engage in repetitive behaviours – including spinning or more persistent barking – especially when placed in more stressful or stimulating environments.
- Obsessive behaviour patterns in general, often linked to higher levels of impulsivity.
- Hypersensitivity to any kind of change in their external environment or normal routine.
- A tendency to react fearfully or aggressively when faced with change, or having change imposed on them.
- Explosive and unpredictable patterns of aggression.
- Obsessive need for control in all contexts.

Note: Chapter Four: *Knowing your Dog's Mind* explains exactly why some more autistic characteristics in Collies predispose them towards particular behaviour problems in later life.

More autistic mental perception in Collies can include a lower ability to read the social intentions of others who suddenly approach. This, in turn, can prompt defensive reactions.

Learning from failure

While many Border Collies may cause few problems, owning a more difficult or problematic dog is not, by any means, unusual. Sometimes it can make you feel very lonely, stemming from a belief that no one else has gone through, or is going through, what you are experiencing with your dog. But I can assure you that you are not alone. In addition, an initial failure, of some kind, with a dog can teach you the most valuable things – not just about dogs but also about yourself, and what you are capable of achieving when something matters enough to you.

Certainly everything of value I have learned about Collies came from the dogs that struggled, or went wrong, or failed in some way or for some reason and needed a lot more help. I will ever be grateful to them, not just for what they taught me, but for what they also inspired me to further discover and learn about the breed in general – much of which is now shared with you in this book series.

So if you are experiencing some sort of problem with your own dog, do not immediately panic, entirely blame yourself, or think you are a useless owner. Do not let emotional despair, or any more personal sense of failure, overwhelm you or paralyse you. Switch on your more logical brain and appreciate the opportunity this affords you to learn and, thereafter, to move on to a better place with your dog – hopefully with the benefit of the advice, and insights laid out in later chapters of this book.

Seeing problems the right way around

Very often, when trying to find answers or solutions to Collie behaviour issues, we are looking at the situation the wrong way around; i.e., what is going on externally, as opposed to what is happening internally, with the dog concerned.

In other words, we focus primarily on the more obvious, outward physical symptoms of a dog's 'problem behaviour' (i.e. lunging and biting, compulsive chasing, shaking with fear, not coming back when called) instead of thinking about how his brain works which, in turn, caused the less desirable behaviour to occur. All physical behaviours in animals can only be as good, or as bad, as the mental state or thought process that launched them.

Our mission therefore, as explored in following chapters, is to work out why a dog's mind feels so compelled to think and react as it does in different situations, and what we can do to change this if reactions in question are less desirable.

When seeking longer-term solutions to any 'problem' dog behaviour, we also need to understand how any dog masters the process of 'change', in terms of his future thinking and behaviour. (*See Understanding and changing the way your Collie thinks.*)

When is your dog's behaviour a 'problem'?

Owners can vary considerably in terms of when they perceive their Collie has a 'problem', or whether his behaviour has become a 'problem' to them. Similarly, some owners will take longer than others to admit that they have a problem in their dog that they cannot solve themselves.

The best definition of when a dog's behaviour needs to be addressed is when it is impacting adversely on the life quality or safety of the owner, or the dog himself, or when it is potentially placing other people or dogs in danger. That is when it is wise to seek professional help; preferably from someone who has extensive knowledge and experience of the Border Collie breed, as Collies can often think and act so differently to other dogs or breeds, as a result of their unique genetic psychology.

A majority of behaviour problems in dogs can be greatly modified, or totally resolved, with the benefit of expert professional help. But do be aware of the part an owner must also play in terms of the retraining that is often involved.

Under no circumstances would I recommend sending your dog away to any 'retraining' establishment where you will not also be present. First, because the very idea that someone would be happy to exclude an owner from a dog's rehabilitation process suggests pretty little respect for the owner(s) concerned. Second, because I have seen some horrendous mental damage done to Collies who have been to places like this.

UNDERSTANDING AND CHANGING THE WAY YOUR COLLIE THINKS

Dogs, like people, get into ingrained habits of thinking and behaving when placed in specific circumstances. These habits can derive from the way a dog is pre-programmed to think and react, genetically. But it can also be a result of what he has learned from past experience and then committed to memory. More often, it is a subtler combination of genetic predisposition and learnt experience.

If a dog does something and keeps repeating it as a mental habit, it is because he is naturally drawn towards such behaviour, and the fact that this behaviour has consistently brought some reward for him in the past. The more of a mental reward the dog gets from the behaviour, the more addictive the behaviour can become.

When we talk of a 'mental reward', we are referring to a hit of 'feel-good' neurochemicals or hormones, such as dopamine or adrenaline (as can be the case with more exhilarating and repetitive physical activities), or some sense in the dog's mind that his behaviour has removed a threat or solved a particular problem for him.

Some behaviours in dogs are easier to change than others, according to how addictive and/or ingrained they have become for the dog in question. It also depends on whether you can offer a reward for different and newer ways of thinking and behaving that is better than the reward he got from his old behaviour. And also whether you can simultaneously make the old behaviour far less rewarding/appealing for him.

Some dogs will only surrender old patterns of thinking and reacting when the consequences of this behaviour become consistently less pleasant or appealing. This is why some 'wrong' behaviours in Collies – including less appropriate chase behaviour and some forms of aggression – may need to be addressed with some kind of deterrent, as well as providing higher value rewards for newer ways of thinking and behaving. See Chapter 9: *Aggression*.

Longer lasting changes in behaviour require the investment of time, patience and psychological insight. PHOTO: CAROL PRICE

If a dog is surrendering old behaviour, which he formerly relied on to keep him 'safe', he may also need more consistent and prolonged reassurance – and experience – that his newer behaviour is equally safe for him.

A dog is ready to change the way he thinks and behaves only as and when his new behaviour proves consistently more rewarding for him than his old behaviour, and he has committed this lesson to his sub-conscious, as well as conscious, mind. For, as outlined in Chapter 7 (*The Instinctive and Impulsive Mind*) and elsewhere in this book, it is the sub-conscious mind that is typically behind most problem behaviours in Collies, and is also the key to their longer-term resolution.

Every dog can also be different in terms of the length of time, and level of retraining, it may take to get him to this point.

Working together: When we work with a dog, and help him to overcome issues, we learn far more of value than from those who always do everything right.
PHOTO: CAROL PRICE

Beware of quick fixes

Similarly, view with suspicion anyone who offers any kind of quick fix to your Collie's problem(s), whether they are a 'whisperer' or a 'listener' or any other kind of self-styled expert.

Dogs – and Border Collies in particular – are far too emotionally intelligent, and psychologically complex to be regarded or treated like this, as any true dog expert knows. Plus, in order to bring about any more meaningful, or longer lasting changes in any dog's behaviour you will need a far more in-depth knowledge of how his brain works.

Frequently I have seen the uniquely complex and sensitive psychology of the Border Collie prove just too testing for people who may otherwise consider themselves dog experts. As a result they write off a dog as a basket case because they cannot sufficiently understand his mind. Alternatively, they try to bludgeon him into more 'obedient' or acceptable behaviours with a far more physically dominating (or bullying) approach. And it is the latter which so often does these dogs great mental harm.

Natural breed variation

What should also be appreciated is the reality that no two Border Collies will ever be completely alike in terms of how they choose to behave. It will always involve some subtle blend, in each case, of genetic aspects, or instincts, that later become expressed in the dog, and the type of learning experiences he has been exposed to throughout his life.

That said, it still helps to have a more precise understanding of the type of personality/behaviour variations that can exist in Border Collies, and assess where your own dog may fall within this wider spectrum of breed traits. In this way you can more successfully gear your future training and handling to his more individual psychology and character.

So we are going to concentrate on this mission in the next chapter.

CHAPTER 2:

THE COLLIE SPECTRUM

Assessing the nature of the dog you own

A breed with many faces: Border Collies can vary immensely, not just in physical looks

I n Book One of this series, *Secrets of the Working Mind,* I explained the reasons why Border Collies vary so much in temperament and behaviour, and how this dated back, genetically, to the breed's earliest founding dogs, over a century ago. For no breed – or the individuals within it – can ever be anything more, or less, than the original genetic material they descended from.

Today's Collies are therefore further permutations, and perpetuations, of the genes contained in their earlier ancestors – for better or worse. There will be genes that govern the way your dog looks, and also genes that will govern the way he is most likely to behave, or view the world around him, even if other earlier rearing, training and learning factors will have some part in this, too.

In order to get a far deeper insight into natural breed variations in Collies, in terms of genetic character and temperament, what will now follow is my Border Collie Spectrum Assessment Process. This is a guide I have devised for owners to pinpoint more accurately where their own dog falls within a range of common breed traits, and specifically those relating to inherent psychology and compulsions, temperament, personality, mental outlook and overall behaviour.

This, in turn, presents a better indication of how easy, or not, your type of Collie may be to live with, or train, or how much external management and support he may need to maintain a better or healthier state of mental balance.

Spectrum ranges and traits

When assessing your own dog on the following spectrum ranges, be aware that the spectrum settings featured – *low, medium, high* – mark opposite extremes and a middle range, for different qualities. Many dogs may fall somewhere in-between these settings, i.e. low to medium, or medium to high.

The 12 key traits I have picked for assessing are as follows:

1. Level of working instinct
2. Level of sensory sensitivity/reactivity
3. Level of mental arousal/self-stimulation
4. Level of obsessional/repetitive activity
5. Speed of learning
6. Level of sociability
7. Level of fearfulness
8. Level of aggressive drive
9. Level of emotional/psychological dependency
10. Tendencies towards manipulative and controlling behaviour
11. Level of impulsivity and impulse control
12. Level of tolerance to change

Once you have judged or marked where your own dog features, with regard to these different spectrum traits, see *Making sense of the results, page 30.*

1. LEVEL OF WORKING INSTINCT

Low	Medium	High

A dog's inherent level of working instinct or drive can often have bearings on how easy he may be to train. However, it is also possible for a dog to have too much working drive, if it translates into more obsessive-compulsive thought processes and behaviours and more sustained levels of mental arousal.

Low working instinct means very little incidence of eye/stalk/chase behaviour in your dog and, similarly, quite low levels of mental intensity/obsessional drive. He may find it harder to maintain consistent focus for any great length of time. He may initially run after a toy but then soon get bored – as opposed to obsessed – with it.

Dogs like these can make far easier pets but less committed workers, and may also be far harder to motivate in training. Compared to a dog with higher working drive, you will need to sustain his attention in much shorter bursts, and reward him far more consistently and excessively.

Medium drive means dogs with a fair level of working instinct, but with a less obsessive edge. They can maintain good levels of mental focus, for longer periods of time, even when continually repeating the same task. They will be happy to train their working focus/instinct on to one selected target – livestock or a toy – rather than scattergun

A Collie's innate level of 'working instinct' may also influence many other aspects of his personality or behaviour.

it more widely around to a range of other moving things. This type of dog can also easily switch his mental intensity/focus off when training ends or his working target is removed.

My own preference is for middle-ranging dogs like these, as I find them easiest to work with, and to live with.

It is still critical, however, that a dog with medium drive has his working mind and instincts disciplined at a young age, and trained on to both yourself and a working target of your choice. Otherwise these instincts – as in higher working drive dogs - could soon escape elsewhere, and on to less appropriate targets, such as traffic, cyclists, runners, birds or that mainstay Collie favourite, other people's footballs.

High working drive holds many benefits in a working or competition dog. However, as earlier stated, it is still possible for a Collie to have just too much working drive, in terms of more extreme mental intensity, energy and neurosis, and more obsessive visual fixations (as outlined in Trait 4) which can be less easy to discipline or re-channel on

to yourself and other chosen outlets. Especially once the dog has selected a preferred obsession target for himself – i.e. anything again from traffic to moving water – and remains stubbornly addicted to it.

People often think the main problem with a pet Collie like this is that "he should be working sheep", when in fact dogs with too much neurotic energy and reactivity, and less ability to self-calm or sustain focus, seldom make very good sheepdogs either. They unsettle livestock, often act too recklessly or impulsively, and/or are rarely calm enough, for long enough, to think clearly, and thus make better decisions when it comes to managing them.

Higher octane dogs like these may find it very hard to switch off, or wind down, even in the face of relatively minor stimulation, which in turn can make them that much harder to live with (also see Trait 3). They can also be far more vulnerable to both over-stimulation and stress. Though it should be noted here that Collies, in general, are vulnerable to the effects of these things, with many otherwise lower drive dogs getting labelled as 'manic' or 'hyper' when they are simply chronically stressed.

2. LEVEL OF SENSORY SENSITIVITY/ REACTIVITY

Low	Medium	High

A dog's inherent levels of sensitivity/reactivity often govern not only how easy he may be to live with, and train, but also how much extra external help, and support, he may need from an owner to stay in a healthier state of mental balance, as also outlined in Trait 3.

Low sensory sensitivity in a Collie is a dog who generally seems far more laid back and less excitable or reactive to any sudden sounds or movements. If you make sudden movements or suddenly raise your voice, he won't immediately leap into action and start mentally buzzing or barking.

He won't become worried or highly vocal/ reactive if you begin to use noisy, moving things like a lawnmower or vacuum cleaner. He will cope better with crowded or noisier environments in general, without showing more obvious signs of tension or unease – such as ears back, lip licking and a more lowered or cowering posture.

He won't be more unduly troubled by things like flashing lights, or the television, or any new source of noise and movement in his environment, which may include anything passing by outside. He is less likely as a result to suffer from serious noise phobias. He is also less likely to indulge in more obsessive-compulsive behaviours revolving round light and movement.

Dogs like these also seem to have fewer reservations about being touched in different parts of their bodies, or about being cuddled or hugged affectionately. For all these reasons they tend to make far easier social companions or pets.

Medium sensory sensitivity in Collies means dogs who have the capacity to be highly excitable, but mostly when faced with set environmental triggers; i.e. any sudden new movements or sounds by an owner, particularly sounds/movements that signal something exciting is about to occur, such as a walk, a game, a chase up the garden, or when a visitor comes to call.

Collies with higher levels of sensory sensitivity and mental excitability may be more prone to phobias and also appear more 'hyper' or 'manic' in nature.

PHOTO: CAROL PRICE

However, they can still develop phobias about louder things such as fireworks or thunderstorms. Unlike dogs with far higher sensory sensitivity, they do seem able to apply some filter – or a more noticeable 'off' switch – to the level of sensory assault they absorb on a daily level, meaning that they are not reacting to every single external source of sensory input all the time. Thus, they find it easier to wind down and relax after exercise or training, as long as surrounding sources of noise/movement – especially by the owner – are kept low.

Dogs like these may still show some unease/apprehension about being touched – particularly their heads and paws – but learn to tolerate it. As they can mix high responsiveness with the ability to subdue their sensory responses when necessary, they are often best for people who want a working or competition dog as well as a social companion.

These dogs, however, can still be in danger of sensory/mental overloading and stress if living or working in environments where sources of external sensory stimulation are too persistent or intense.

High sensory sensitivity in Collies applies to dogs who appear to be mentally buzzing most of the time, in reaction to any form of external sensory stimulation, such as light, sound, or movement. This is a mental state we would tend to classify, all in all, as 'neurotic' or 'hyper'. This type of dog may also exhibit more autistic traits in general, i.e. persistently self stimulate and indulge in obsessive patterns of behaviour (also see Traits 3 and 4).

Sensory super-sensitive dogs may also find being approached suddenly, or being physically touched, quite unnerving. They may try to avoid being grabbed or held, shake or tremble when you try to groom them, or even become aggressive through panic. They may also be far more likely to develop noise phobias, including phobias about particular household devices or machines.

When training a dog like this, you must use an exceptionally light touch, and never show any sign of frustration, disapproval or impatience. Otherwise very soon he could develop highly negative associations with the whole training process, and mentally shut down, or even freeze, whenever you ask him to do something for you.

3. LEVEL OF MENTAL AROUSAL

Low	Medium	High

Often related to levels of sensory sensitivity in dogs, what is meant by the level of 'mental arousal' in Collies is how quickly they will enter a more hyper-aroused or excitable mental state, how long it is sustained, and how long it takes them to wind down again.

Low mental arousal levels in Collies means dogs that do not readily enter a more agitated/aroused mental state in reaction to external triggers such as light, sound or movement. In general they retain a calmer demeanour and it takes far more in the way of external stimulation or provocation to raise them into states of noticeably higher excitement or anxiety.

As Collies get older, their mental arousal mechanisms – along with their sensory faculties – can often become less acute, meaning they do not react so strongly as they might have done, in the past, to some external stimuli. Dogs suffering from more severe forms of mental 'burnout', as a result of persistent past sensory/psychological over-arousal, can react in a similar way, or seem, in general, more noticeably depressed or withdrawn.

Medium level of mental arousal means dogs that still have the capacity to enter more excitable mental states in response to external stimuli, but are able to exert better control over this process. This relates to how speedily they will 'wind up' and also how speedily they can 'wind down' again. This is a result of genetic factors – which can play a significant part – but also far better training in impulse control when the dog was younger, as covered in Book Two of this series.

High levels of mental arousal in Collies is typified by dogs that need very little in the way of external stimulation to enter higher states of excitement or anxiety, or just noticeably more 'manic' or agitated behaviour. Moreover, once aroused in this way, they can sustain this heightened mental state for considerable periods of time. Typically, this type of dog will be constantly fidgeting, running around or looking for additional sources of sensory

Dogs with less extreme arousal mechanisms usually find it easier to maintain focus in work, training or competition.

stimulation within his immediate environment in order to maintain his higher mental arousal levels. This could involve eyeing or chasing shadows or dust, batting around food or water bowls, barking and whining, licking himself or other surfaces or constantly pestering his owner to give him toys or play with him.

In human autistics, such behaviour is known as 'stimming', or more persistent self-stimulation. We often view the continually 'hyper' behaviour it produces in a dog as a problem in itself, as opposed to being a symptom of a rather bigger issue. This is the dog's inability to keep his own mental arousal mechanisms under better control. Dogs like these

will also struggle to stop emotions such as fear, frustration, anxiety or aggression exploding into more extreme physical responses and will be exposed to far more stress, as a result, throughout their lifetimes.

The mental vulnerabilities of dogs like these need to be better understood. Similarly, they benefit most from living environments with the least amount of external sensory pressure (see Chapter 10 on *Sensory Detox* for more advice on this). They will also need far more help in learning to self calm, and to master greater impulse control, as well as being given more positive outlets for their mental energies (*as outlined in Book Two*).

4. LEVEL OF OBSESSIONAL/ REPETITIVE ACTIVITY

Low	Medium	High

Dogs with more obsessional – or even obsessive compulsive – patterns of behaviour may also have higher levels of working instinct (Trait 1) or poorer levels of impulse control (Trait 11) as frequently these characteristics go together, in terms of their degree of intensity.

Low levels of obsessional activity means dogs with a far lower compulsion to keep repeating the same patterns of behaviour, over and over again. Typically this behaviour will revolve around some kind of eyeing, stalking, chasing or circling activity, with regard to something that moves, or the dog anticipates is about to move. Dogs like these may also be far more laid back in general and be less prone to a range of different neuroses or phobias. They often make easier pets, but somewhat less driven or committed workers.

Medium levels of obsessional activity means dogs whose patterns of the above type of behaviour can be more easily subdued or controlled on command, especially if they were also better trained in impulse control when younger. In other words, their levels of mental intensity/working drive have a more noticeable 'off' switch. Dogs like these tend to make the best workers – be this in livestock work or different forms of canine competition – because they combine a higher level of obsessive drive with a counterbalancing degree of impulse control. Both components are essential in any good working dog.

High levels of obsessional/repetitive behaviour results in behaviour that is more intense and continuous, and which owners might find far harder to stop. It often signifies a more autistic mind. As such, it may be driven by more overwhelming compulsions that the dog himself will also struggle to control. It is vital to spot this tendency as early as possible before it develops into more dangerous endeavours, such as chasing traffic or trains. Dogs like these can also often be troubled by more intense social anxieties, and/or a range of other different phobias or neuroses.

The key requirements for these dogs are firstly to identify one sole legitimate target on to which the dog can unleash his obsessive compulsions, i.e., in the absence of livestock, a toy that you can control. Then, secondly, you need to work, simultaneously, on improving the dog's overall levels of impulse control, which can also govern how he responds to sensations like anxiety or frustration. The latter will also be critical in gaining ever better control of your dog's behaviour. Both of these issues were covered in Book Two of this series, but also see Trait 11 and Chapter 7: *The Instinctive and Impulsive Mind.*

Collies can target obsessive and repetitive eyeing/stalking/ chasing behaviours on to basically anything that moves. This could include toys and household objects, such as brooms, to dust, leaves, water, lights and shadows.

PHOTO: CAROL PRICE

5. SPEED OF LEARNING

Low	Medium	High

It is commonly said that Collies are 'easy to train' when, really, they are just fast learners. It's important to make this distinction, as a dog who is a fast learner is just as capable of learning the wrong lesson as quickly as the right one. Moreover, another quirk about Collies is that once they have learned something, and ingrained it, they can often be quite stubborn about changing it again. Thus for all these reasons *(and as outlined in Book Two of this series)* taking better control of your dog's whole learning process, from as early in his life as possible, can be critical.

However, Collies may still vary considerably in the speed with which they learn and commit different lessons to memory.

Low speed of learning in a Collie means a dog who may need to be taught, or trained, the same lesson many times before he eventually ingrains it. Owners may get very frustrated with dogs who seem less able to retain previously taught lessons, or exercises, or even mistake this for more wilful 'disobedience', when it is not. It is simply a quirk of the dog's mind or brain that he cannot help. Dogs like these need a lot more patience and persistence from owners, together with a greater understanding of their problem.

Medium speed of learning means a dog who may initially learn something fairly fast, but who will then need the lesson to be persistently rewarded/reinforced for some while after – and in a multitude of different contexts – before it eventually becomes more reliably ingrained in his mind. Collies can vary quite considerably in this respect.

High speed of learning means a dog who picks up new lessons or exercises extremely fast, and also commits them to memory with the same level of speed. Dogs like these can be a dream to train. But in their overall speed of learning, you have to be careful that they are not also learning some bad habits, without you realising it, until these become equally ingrained. This is because the connections they make between an action and a mental reward can often occur so rapidly that you might not even notice it happening. That is, until the dog keeps repeating a less desired behaviour you hadn't intended him to learn.

The ability to focus has a major impact on the ability to learn new behaviours.

6. LEVEL OF SOCIABILITY

Low	Medium	High

A dog's inherent level of sociability often governs how easy or not he may be to live with as a social companion, as follows:

Some Collies are naturally less socially aware or outgoing, as individuals, and will need far more help to build greater social confidence and tolerance.

PHOTO: CAROL PRICE

Low: The lowest social extreme in Collies can be dogs who become virtually – or actually – agoraphobic, i.e. so averse to new people, dogs, sights, sounds, etc., that their world progressively shrinks. The parameters of what these dogs can cope with become restricted to the familiar home environment – or even just one place they regard as 'safest' in the home environment. This could be under a table or on a landing, the latter enabling the dog to better view/evade any potential new threat coming into the home environment via the front door.

Dogs like these can often be more autistic in mind-set, and at the heart of their problem lie other traits consistent with this, such as poorer social recognition and awareness, a higher degree of sensory sensitivity (Trait 2) and fearfulness (Trait 7), and a more acute intolerance to newer or stranger things (see Trait 12).

Some dogs with lower social confidence, due to these inherent issues, may initially go out for a walk but then remain in a state of high anxiety – or even panic – throughout. A dog may be forever pulling on the lead, panting heavily, to rush forward the moment when he can return to the safety of the car or the familiarity of his home environment. He may also appear exceptionally hyper-alert, or begin lunging at passing dogs, people, or traffic, in a bid to displace his inner tension, anxiety and stress.

It is incredibly important to understand the process whereby – without more insightful handling, or a fuller appreciation of the kind of mind you are dealing with – a Collie's social confidence can rapidly implode, from puppyhood onwards. Thus the kind of training and socialising you must undertake to avoid this was outlined in Book Two of this series. Chapter 8 of this book also covers the issue of fear in Collies more widely.

Moderate sociability in Collies can mean dogs that are fine with people/dogs they know well, particularly from earlier puppyhood, but who may become progressively more reserved, or appear indifferent, when meeting any newer person/dog as they grow older. It is actually quite common for Collies to become more socially reserved, the older they get.

Sometimes this is due to a more natural decline in social curiosity, as the dog gets older, but it can also be down to owners devoting less energy or effort to socialising an older dog, and inviting him to keep forging new relationships, than they would a puppy.

Lowered social curiosity or interest in Collies of this kind only becomes a bigger problem if the dog gets more aggressive in his desire to keep newer people or dogs out of his space, because he finds their 'newness' more psychologically threatening to him in some way. Note: Aggression in Collies will be covered in Chapter 9 of this book.

High sociability means a supremely confident dog, very friendly and outgoing in his interactions with any new person or dog he meets. Dogs like these are natural charmers and are a pleasure to own. The only potential downside is greater recklessness, on their part, when approaching less sociable dogs – or people – either of which may be a source of conflict, or a snappier exchange.

7. LEVEL OF FEARFULNESS

Low	Medium	High

As outlined in more detail in Chapter 8: *Fear and its Fallout*, there are very many reasons why Collies can become fearful of different things, including the nature of their own more particular, or personal, 'fear settings', which can often begin with elements of genetic predisposition.

Low fearfulness in Collies refers to dogs that are just inherently more confident and readily accepting of newer sights, sounds, experiences, people, dogs etc., out of an essential belief that most new things are worth trusting. Dogs like these tend to make easy-going and adaptable social companions.

Medium fearfulness in Collies means dogs that show mild apprehension towards most new things, from which they soon recover. However, a dog of this type may still exhibit more extreme fear reactions towards specific things, such as thunder, fireworks or just someone or something that he perceives as a potential threat. As these responses can be so instinctive, or primal, you won't always be able to predict what may trigger them.

High fearfulness in Collies (also see *Level of sociability, page 24*) results in dogs with extremely low social tolerance and on-going anxieties or phobias about a large number of things in their environment.

Commonly, dogs like these – that may, once again, have more extreme autistic edges to their personalities – will be excessive in their fear response (i.e. shaking, shivering, panting), and they will take far longer to recover. They are also more likely to believe that anything new they encounter is a threat. These dogs need an awful lot of external support and can often be quite stressful to own. But, as ever, they cannot help the way they are made. These issues will be covered in more depth in Chapter 8: *Fear and its Fallout*.

Shrinking their world: Collies who are more fearful by nature may seek out favourite 'hiding' spots when anxious, or have greater struggles dealing with life beyond the more familiar home environment.

PHOTO: CAROL PRICE

8. LEVEL OF AGGRESSIVE DRIVE

Low	Medium	High

As outlined more fully in Chapter 9, other than in a purely predatory context, aggression in Collies – as in most dogs – is generally inspired by deeper feelings of fear, anxiety, frustration or insecurity that then seek some physical release. How readily or not a dog will resort to aggression, however, can still vary considerably in individual dogs, according to many different factors, both genetic and learned.

Low aggressive drive in Collies means dogs that need excessive external provocation in order to mount a defensive aggressive response. Alternatively, even with such excessive provocation, a dog of this type may still choose not to be aggressive. It is a total myth that *any* or every dog can, or will, be aggressive, given the right circumstances or provocation. Some dogs will always opt for flight or freeze reactions, even when exceptionally provoked or threatened.

Medium aggressive drive means Collies that may need a higher level of external provocation in order to launch a defensive aggressive response, but who, in the main, are not aggressive.

High aggressive drive in Collies means dogs that need very little in the way of external provocation in order to become aggressive. They may also be *offensively* aggressive towards other people and dogs.

Dogs like these usually suffer from the additional trait of poorer impulse control in general (see Trait 11), making it harder for them to inhibit their physical reactions to emotional sensations, such as fear of frustration. As such, they will always need exceptionally careful handling (*as outlined more fully in Chapter 9: Aggression*) if they are not to become dangerous.

Aggression in Collies is often less well understood — including why some dogs are more prone to this behaviour than others.

PHOTO: CAROL PRICE

9. LEVEL OF EMOTIONAL/ PSYCHOLOGICAL DEPENDENCY

Low	Medium	High

Many Collies become readily attached – if not *over* **attached – not just to their owners but also humans in general, both psychologically and emotionally** *(a phenomenon more fully explained in Chapter 6 on Separation issues).* **Others may be far more independent or even aloof. Both extremes may present some future issues for owners to deal with, as follows:**

Low emotional dependency in a Collie means a dog that seems far less needy of human, or owner, presence. On walks he will happily rush way ahead, entertaining himself, without ever double checking to see where you are. He may have a very poor recall. He does not seem particularly bothered whether you are pleased with him or displeased with him. It can be hard to both get, and keep, his attention in training.

Often, a dog like this is far less owner dependent because he suffers from greater social disconnection in general, i.e. a lower ability to relate to others on a social level. He will tend not to mind his own company at home, and will not always be checking to see where you are or what you are doing.

Such dogs will need a lot more work put into their training, especially when it comes to exercises relating to recall and maintaining owner focus. This type of dog will also require you to work harder on both building and maintaining a working bond. Also see Chapter 5 on *Less responsive dogs.*

Medium emotional dependency in Collies means dogs that may be happy to go some way ahead of you on a walk, but will keep checking, every so often, to see where you are. They will have a fairly good recall, though not always instant.

With this type of dog, it is not unduly hard to get his attention in training. He will not like your disapproval. At home, he will be happy to stay in one place far longer than a more dependent dog before checking where you are. He will not constantly follow you around. He may show apprehension about being left alone when you go out but – unlike a more highly dependent dog – will not exhibit intense distress, or become more hysterical with relief when you return home.

High emotional dependency in Collies results in dogs that seem pretty much addicted to their owners' presence. A dog with high emotional dependency will constantly crave attention and approval. Any disapproval from his owner causes him immense distress. He will follow you from room to room to see where you are and what you are doing. He will become anxious at the slightest sign that you might be going out and leaving him. He will greet you hysterically when you return home.

Owner fixated: Higher emotional dependency in a Collie may give you a seemingly more loyal and devoted companion — but also one who copes less well when separated from you.
PHOTO: CAROL PRICE

He may also persistently lie in places such as hallways, the bottom of the stairs, or before the front door, in order that he can keep an even better eye on your movements or possible departures. On a walk he will stay constantly close to you. He has a superb recall. It is easy to both get, and keep, his attention in training.

Obviously dogs like these may have many benefits for an owner, but the downside remains the more intense level of stress the dog will experience whenever separated from his owner, or other more reassuring human presence. *(Once again see Chapter 6 for more on this).*

Moreover, there may be several other common Collie neuroses, or compulsions, driving a dog's need to keep his owner in sight at all times, including those revolving around a more constant need to preserve sameness, and those exhibiting a more persistent need to maintain control.

10. TENDENCIES TOWARDS MANIPULATIVE AND CONTROLLING BEHAVIOUR

Low	Medium	High

In Book One of this series, I explained how the desire to both defend and control personal space – as well as anything or anyone that may be present on the periphery – can run deep in many Collies. Although an asset in their livestock working past, a by-product of this trait can be a dog with a more manipulative and controlling nature, as follows:

Low manipulative and controlling tendencies in Collies means dogs quite at ease with other people/dogs etc. coming into their space. A dog of this type will not immediately try to take charge of any social interaction with other dogs or people. He will not persistently use pressure tactics or pester power (i.e. nudging, barking, whining, pawing) to better control his owner, or make him/her do what he wants them to do.

Medium manipulative/controlling tendencies means dogs less able to resist the chance to take control of their owners, or other dogs, in any social context, but that only employ this behaviour when the opportunity more readily presents itself, i.e. it is less of an obsessive daily pastime.

A dog of this type may use staring, whining, barking or pawing at his owner's legs to hold their attention, or make them do something such as feed him, walk him or play with him. He may use the same tactics to stop an owner interacting for too long with another person or dog, when out on a walk, or when you are talking on the phone. His manipulation strategies, however, are entirely psychological. He will never use aggression as a tool of control.

High manipulative/controlling tendencies means dogs who are far more obsessive in their need to control their environment, plus other people, dogs – and their owner(s). They may seek to immediately take charge of any encounter they have with other dogs, which may include using aggression.

A dog of this type may try to totally monopolise and control visitors to the home, with attention-seeking strategies, such as jumping up or constantly whining and pawing, demanding to be petted. Alternatively he may become more aggressive in his control of visitors and their movements.

Like medium controlling dogs, if an owner stops to talk to another person on a walk, this type of dog may constantly use pressurising tactics, such as whining, barking, jumping up or even nipping, to get the attention back on himself and get his owner moving again. However, he may also become aggressive if he owner pays undue attention to other dogs.

At home, he may also try to take control of strategic household territories, such as the front door, hallway, or top of the stairs, and become aggressive if people try to move him. Dogs like these may need to be handled with particular care if they are not to become dangerous. *This is covered more fully in Chapter 9 on Aggression.*

Arch controllers: Collies can be extraordinarily adept at manipulating owners to do what they want, through any variety of pressure tactics, including staring, pawing, barking or whining.

11. LEVEL OF IMPULSIVITY AND IMPULSE CONTROL

Low	Medium	High

The trait of higher impulsivity – or poorer impulse control – is thought to be highly significant in dogs, in terms of how it may be linked to a range of more reactive behaviours in them, including aggression. A dog's impulsivity levels basically govern how well, or not, his brain can inhibit the process of emotional sensations turning into physical reactions. This includes the way he physically responds to emotions such as excitement, frustration, anxiety or fear.

Low impulsivity – or higher impulse control – usually gives you a pretty laid back dog. He is generally less excitable in nature and not easily provoked into a more aggressive response. He also copes more calmly in situations where other dogs may find it far harder to contain feelings of frustration or anxiety (i.e. whining, barking, jumping, entering a far more aroused and agitated mental state). Some dogs can have better impulse control when it comes to the use of aggression, but poorer impulse control when it comes to how easily they can be provoked into a more fearful or excitable mental and physical state. Typically such differences will have a genetic root.

Medium impulsivity means dogs that, in the main, can learn – or be trained – to master better impulse control over all aspects of their behaviour. However, such dogs may still have certain triggers which make the struggle to contain their reactions noticeably harder for them. It is really important to keep working on the focus/impulse control levels of dogs like these to avoid them developing more reactive behaviour patterns, in general, that spiral ever further out of control.

High impulsivity, or poorer impulse control, means dogs far less able to control their physical reactions to a range of external emotional/mental/sensory triggers. As such, a dog may be a more agitated/excitable individual in general and respond more excessively to sources of sound and movement. But a bigger problem will usually be his use of aggression, if his own form of poorer impulse control affects how readily he will display this kind of reaction, or behaviour.

Dogs like these may develop patterns of lunge-nip behaviour on the lead when approached by other passing dogs or people. They can also be prone to more sudden eruptions of aggression; often appearing to occur with little pre-warning. The dog may seem pretty 'normal', or even fairly submissive one moment, and the next his eyes and body may suddenly appear to 'freeze', which will rapidly be followed by a more explosive aggressive outburst.

Shorter fuses: Dogs with inherently poorer impulse control will find it harder to keep more excitable reactions in check.
PHOTO: CAROL PRICE

Often the dog may have one particular target for this behaviour; i.e. newer dogs or people, children, or visitors to the home. But sometimes the problem can spread out to include owners as well, in situations where the dog suddenly feels more immediately threatened. That is why the problem should always be taken very seriously, from the moment it first presents itself. *Note: There will be far more advice on dogs like these in Chapter 9 on Aggression.*

Interestingly – although not necessarily surprising – students at the University of Lincoln's School of Life Sciences, in the UK, did a study of impulsivity levels in Border Collies and found that higher impulsivity/poorer impulse control was significantly more common in Collies from working lines, as opposed to those from show bred lines.

12. LEVEL OF TOLERANCE TO CHANGE

Low	Medium	High

How tolerant or not a dog may be to any kind of change within his normal routines, or surrounding environment, can often have bearings on other aspects of his behaviour, requiring greater mental flexibility or adaptability, including many different social or training scenarios.

Low fear or intolerance of change in Collies means dogs that are far more mentally accommodating to all manner of newer or stranger experiences or events. A dog of this type will tend to be more naturally outgoing and confident as a dog, and trust that most new things he is exposed to will not harm him. Dogs like these tend to be a lot easier to own. However, they are probably less common within the Collie breed than dogs with more cautious approaches to change.

Medium intolerance of change in Collies will give you dogs that may still have some apprehensions about newer events or experiences, but their reactions to them will be less extreme. A dog of this type will be better able to over-ride any original panic surge caused by a newer or stranger event, and similarly keep any responses related to this under better control.

Similarly he will recover from initial aversions to anything 'newer' much quicker, rather than letting them become ingrained.

Sometimes the essential difference between a Collie who has lower, or rather better, tolerance of change will not just be genetic, but also down to how well he was socialised, and socially trained and stretched, when he was younger.

High intolerance of change means dogs who can become more highly disturbed or unnerved by even the most minor change in their usual routine or external environment. Typical examples include being asked to eat or try a new food, sleep in a new place or even having to walk on a different side to you, on the lead, or sit in a place in the car that is different to where they normally sit.

The problem arises from the dog's inner – and more primal – mental wiring that reads such changes as potentially threatening. Being a more instinctive impulse, or reaction, also be aware that it is not something the dog is able to fully rationalise in his mind, prior to reacting – as we might - or find easy to consciously control.

Generally you may find that dogs with this trait may need their daily lives and routines 'micro-managed' to a far higher degree – in terms of the constant perpetuation of 'sameness' – if they are not to display more intensely anxious or agitated behaviour. However, the downside of this approach is that you then have a dog whose levels of social tolerance shrink ever inwards, when they need to be stretched ever outwards for the sake of his greater psychological health.

Often dogs with a greater addiction to 'sameness' are mistaken for dogs that are too emotionally attached to their owners (as highlighted under Trait 9, earlier), and this is the reason given why they cope so badly when left alone. But often this separation distress is caused less by emotional over-attachment *per se*, and more by the traumatic loss of sameness an owner's sudden absence represents in the dog's mind. More on this issue, again, in Chapter 6 on *Separation issues*.

Making sense of the results

Hopefully this chapter, and this Border Collie Spectrum Assessment Process, will give you a far clearer picture of the more individual nature of the Collie you own, and the essential traits and mental components that, when combined together, build his overall character.

All in all, the existence of such a character spectrum further reinforces the injustice we do dogs, as a whole, in relating to them as if they are all much the same inside, when even dogs within the same breed can be so very different to each other in so many ways.

The Collie Spectrum thus highlights not only the more intense variability of Collies, as individuals, but also the tendency of some qualities in these dogs to go hand in hand. For example, *high* working instinct, *high* sensory sensitivity/reactivity and an equally higher capacity for more obsessive or controlling

Something is different! Collies can be hypersensitive to any changes in their normal daily routines or living environment and may react to these with greater restlessness and anxiety — or finding a 'safer' space to hide.
PHOTO: CAROL PRICE

behaviour patterns. Or sometimes one characteristic in a dog may lead more inevitably to another, such as *lower* impulse control and *higher* aggressive drive or *higher* levels of mental arousal/reactivity. Or *lower* tolerance of change and *higher* fearfulness.

But mostly what I would like readers, and owners, to glean from this Border Collie Spectrum Assessment Process – especially those considering their own Collies to be somewhat 'abnormal' – is how incredibly broad the range for relatively 'normal' behaviour within the breed can be. By homing in on the inherent qualities that characterise our dogs, as individuals, or those that give us greater problems with them, we are already on the first step to dealing with them in a better way. This is so much better than wasting any time blaming our dogs for what they cannot change about themselves.

Having looked at the deeper reasons why Collies behave as they do, there always remains a difference between behaviour in a dog that has a more fixed and sustained pattern, over time, and that which seems to change more suddenly – which is what we will be looking at in the next chapter.

CHAPTER 3:

WORSENING BEHAVIOURS

Reasons for changes in your dog's behaviour

A Border Collie's behaviour can change at any time, either suddenly or more gradually. Sometimes the reasons are fairly obvious, at other times they may require much deeper investigation.

When a dog is not behaving as we would like him to, it is in the nature of humans to think: "how can I *make* him behave like this or that?" Instead we should be thinking "what is *stopping* him from being able to behave in a more desirable/appropriate manner?" You will also find yourself asking: "why can't he just behave like 'other' dogs?" Which is a good question, to which you will need to find the answer.

More sudden changes in behaviour

Most more serious behaviour problems in Collies tend not to occur, or develop, overnight. As outlined in the next chapter, they have a tendency, instead, to be rooted more deeply in your dog's genetic psychology, and most commonly will come to light, or worsen – without better help, or training – as the dog gets older.

If, by contrast, your dog seems to change his behaviour suddenly, and begins acting in a way that seems very different to his 'normal character', then the best first step is to get him thoroughly checked over by a vet. For anything from a persistent pain source or illness to a range of hormonal or metabolic disorders could be the central cause of this change in behaviour.

Pain or illness can place the body and mind of any dog under excessive stress, and thereafter this will be externalised via changes in his behaviour, including higher levels of reactivity or increased 'grumpiness'.

Other signs that a dog could be experiencing pain or feel less well include:

- Greater lethargy or less interest and energy when it comes to his more normal reactions or routines.
- Unusual digging and stretching behaviour in the home or garden, as dogs often do this to displace internal discomfort, particularly pain related to the abdomen, neck, shoulders or spine.
- The dog repeatedly rubbing or pawing his face or muzzle or scratching or shaking his ears – a potential source of toothache or earache
- Lying or sleeping in less usual places in the home, other than his normal bed.

- Also note that Collies in persistent pain can sometimes react in a far more excitable way, as a displacement strategy, or because the pain seems less acute to them once their adrenaline levels rise

Medications and diet

If your dog's change in behaviour coincided with some change in his diet, or when prescribed some new medication, these could also be a factor.

Some Collies can have more unusual reactions to even commonly prescribed canine drugs, due to their uniquely sensitive neurochemistry. This includes making them more agitated and reactive.

Be particularly alert to artificial additives or colourings in your dog's food, treats or medication. Try to eliminate these entirely from his food or treats. If you suspect a certain medication is affecting your dog's behaviour adversely, discuss changing this with your vet.

If you keep a close check on your dog's behaviour you will be able to pick up signs of stress or discomfort at an early stage.

Neutering and spaying

Neutering or spaying can also result in subsequent changes in the mental outlook, or behaviour, of dogs. This is due to plummeting levels of sex hormones, which may be more intrinsically linked to the dog's inner levels of confidence or mental wellbeing than is often considered.

Neutering and spaying, and the pros and cons of such procedures for dogs, is the subject of many varying views and opinions, among both owners and vets alike. However when people airily state – as they often do – that neutering or spaying dogs *never* makes any difference to their behaviour, it simply isn't true. You can't drastically alter the hormonal balances present in any animal, and expect it to have zero impact on the way they subsequently behave.

Human females know they are having a menopause because of the significantly different way they begin to feel, or think, or behave, when levels of oestrogen start to plummet. Similarly human males with lower testosterone levels are far more prone to anxiety and depression – and grumpiness! And none of this is a coincidence.

Quite a few studies have also noted behavioural changes found in dogs post spaying/neutering, which include higher levels of social reserve, or fearfulness or fear-based aggression. These may take up to a year after neutering/spaying surgery to become most evident, as hormone levels decline.

This is not to say that all dogs will be similarly affected, in terms of their behaviour, by neutering or spaying; it could still be the best course of action for your own dog. It remains a very personal issue and decision for every owner, and may also be related to specific life circumstances. But owners also need to know of the potential behavioural downsides of these procedures on dogs.

A dog may reveal new aspects of his personality as he goes through adolescence.

Early operations

Sometimes people insist that spaying/neutering has not changed their dog's personality or behaviour in any way, while overlooking how early on in life many dogs may have these operations – sometimes even before puberty.

What this means is that owners never get the opportunity to discover how different their dog's adult personality/behaviour might have been if he/she had not been neutered/spayed, and had instead gone through a more natural adolescence, followed by a more natural developmental journey into their full adult identity. So there is no truer, or more accurate, comparison left to be made.

It is also why more effective comparisons between how a dog behaves prior to and after neutering or spaying are best seen in dogs who have these operations when they are older (i.e. three to four years plus).

So sometimes neutering or spaying may change dogs for the better, and at other times not. It depends entirely on how much sex hormone levels – as opposed to countless other factors – were influencing the dog's behaviour for the worse. It could also be argued that the adolescence process itself – as opposed to the spaying and neutering operations that are typically performed around this time – is what mostly brings flaws in a dog's intrinsic temperament or character to the fore.

My abiding concern, however, is that less favourable behaviour changes such surgery can bring about in dogs are either too readily dismissed, or not always sufficiently discussed, or explored, with owners prior to the operation taking place. This means they are less prepared for them if they happen.

Changes triggered by adolescence

There is no doubt that adolescence – which in dogs can be an age period ranging from about five to 18 months – is a major watershed moment in the lives of all animals. Hormonally, physically, neurologically and psychologically, so much is in the process of flux and growth and change inside them, as they make the fuller transition to their adult identities, and leave infancy behind.

Such a wider upheaval process can also trigger some more significant changes in your Collie's behaviour. These may include behaviours you may consider more worrying and new, when they are often just the more intense adult expression of deeper genetic qualities in your dog that were always there. These could be tendencies towards greater fearfulness, or aggressive behaviour – especially towards stranger people or dogs – as well as more controlling or control resistant behaviour, and more obsessive or neurotic working patterns or traits.

Sometimes these changes can come as a bit of a shock for owners, who will say of their now more wayward teenage dogs: "but she/he was so nice as a puppy...", much as parents will say how lovely their children were before they became teenagers. Adolescence in dogs is something of a developmental lottery, in that you can't always know what a puppy is going to be like as an adult, until he has come through this process to the other side. However, quality of breeding, as ever, will play a major part in this.

In the human world, it is recognised that 75 per cent of all psychological disorders only occur in people around, or more immediately post, adolescence. This is why, during your dog's adolescent period, you should be vigilant to any changes in his behaviour that you think could become a bigger problem later – particularly increased nervousness/aggression – and get professional help for it right away. Do not wait for it to become a major issue, or imagine he will "just grow out of it" without expert help. Because he won't.

There is a difference, however, between sensibly anticipating potentially more serious problems in growing dogs, and becoming so fraught with worry and anxiety at the prospect that you forget that elements of greater independence, unresponsiveness, and downright unruliness are pretty common in adolescent dogs. If not a more essential part of the brief.

Being better prepared

Of course, not all Collies change for the worse around adolescence and beyond. Indeed, many sail through this period, and remain remarkably

The ageing process can bring about mental and behavioural, as well as physical, changes in your dog.
PHOTO: CAROL PRICE

well adjusted, especially if you stick to the kind of training and on-going social guidance previously outlined in Book Two of this series. But once again this is a question of owners being, or feeling, prepared for any changes that might come in their teenage dogs, understanding why this happens, and knowing what to do about it.

By better understanding how adolescence can change the nature of a dog – through greatly exacerbating any genetic tendencies that were already in him – the less impressed you will be when the breeder takes no responsibility, stating: "he was fine when he left me as a puppy". Because it's the kind of dog a puppy becomes *after* adolescence that mostly reflects the overall quality of his genetic temperament and character, not the kind of dog he may have been before that transition occurred.

Stress caused by 'change'

Previously in this book series I have outlined how excessively sensitive many Collies can be to 'change' of any kind, in their normal living circumstances, or daily routines. In some dogs, in fact, even the most relatively minor alteration in their normal daily routine can be sufficient to induce considerable anxiety.

This is again a quirk of the Collie psychology, whereby the persistence of 'sameness' is equated with mental reassurance and security in the dog's mind. But change – however small – is more readily equated with threat, which is why it subsequently inspires feelings of greater anxiety and stress.

In my experience, the Collie that shows autistic traits in other ways (as detailed in Chapter 1, *Understanding more autistic patterns of behaviour in your dog*, and also earlier books in this series), will react adversely to change of any kind. The change in question could be anything from some minor alteration in his normal diet to asking him to sleep in a different place, or having visitors to stay, or workmen in the house.

So if your Collie's behaviour, again, suddenly seems to change for the worse, and he appears more agitated and anxious than usual, consider whether this could be directly related to any change in his normal life circumstances or daily routines. No matter how minor such changes may appear to you, the change in question may hold the key to his altered behaviour.

If you are able to reverse this change, and your dog returns to a happier or more balanced mental state, clearly this alteration is what brought about the knock-on effects on his behaviour. If you are not able to reverse it, or would prefer not to, then be aware of how much longer it can take some Collies to come to terms, mentally, with such an assault on their need for 'sameness'. As a rule, Collies always cope better with any change phased in more gradually, and subtly, rather than imposed on them more suddenly, which it can help to be better aware of.

Age related changes

The ageing process can bring about mental, as well as physical, changes in your Collie. Sometimes the two are related, in that when older dogs suffer on-going discomfort from things like arthritis in their joints or spine, this invariably affects their overall mood, and they may seem generally more retiring or even grumpier in their everyday behaviour. In such circumstances it is always worth checking with your vet to see what treatments may make them more comfortable.

Older dogs may also become far 'clingier' around their owners, or more anxious than they were, when younger, at the prospect of any change in their normal environment or routines. Additionally, whereas some Collies may master greater impulse control as they get older, others may more progressively lose it, as a result of the ageing process. This means that they more readily enter an agitated or anxious state – typically exhibited in more persistent barking or whining – or could become snappier with others who invade their space.

When you have an older Collie it is important to be alert to any sudden change in his behaviour that could suggest a more serious underlying health problem, and also be as patient and kind as possible, in the wake of his increasing level of vulnerability. Some owners do not always find it easy to accept that their dog is getting older, and thus when he is in need of greater comfort and compassion, as well as greater peace and rest, and a cutting back on his previous levels of activity. It is likely that your dog gave you all he could during his prime years of life and, in older age, it is pay back time, when you should look after him as sympathetically and insightfully as you can for the time he has left.

CHAPTER 4:

KNOWING YOUR DOG'S MIND

Key traits driving common Collie behavioural issues

The mind of a dog may seem an invisible thing to us on the outside, but inside it lie the answers to everything he does.
PHOTO: CAROL PRICE

Having covered more sudden changes in the way Collies behave, and why these commonly occur, this chapter is going to look at behaviour issues in the breed that are more rooted in the dog's whole genetic psychology. In other words, the tendency for the dog to have these issues was always there, waiting for the appropriate trigger, including adolescence, as covered in the last chapter. It is just that an owner might never have realised this.

Whenever I meet any Collie for the first time, I am never just looking at his outward self. I am looking, instead, at the mind inside the dog; more exactly the kind of mind it is, and the part it will play in orchestrating his whole behaviour.

Is it, for instance, a more stable, trusting and balanced mind, allowing the dog to behave in a relaxed, healthy and sociable way? Or is it a more turbulent, agitated and untrusting mind, inspiring far more fearful and anxious behaviour? Or a more acutely sensitive mind, easily wounded by any number of surrounding sensory assaults? Or a mind with poorer impulse control and thus prone to more reactive, obsessive and compulsive patterns of behaviour, which the dog is less able to consciously contain? And is the dog keen to openly engage with other dogs and people, or much happier to remain cocooned in his own more personal and limited little mental world?

Of course, countless different factors will always play their part in shaping a dog's behaviour, but it all starts with the basic kind of genetic mind he was born with.

Seeing the mind

The mind of a dog may seem a totally invisible thing to us, on the outside. But inside, in all its wealth of brain cells, and chemical and electrical reactions, lies the source of every thought your dog has and every action he performs. Some canine brains, or minds, are programmed to work differently to others which, in turn, so often explains why they may inspire very different types of behaviour, too.

Often, when owners tell me that they wish their Collie would behave differently, what they really mean is that they wish he had a different – and perhaps rather less challenging – kind of dog brain.

Which, in turn, might make their own life with him a bit easier.

However, a Collie can only have the kind of mind, or brain, he was born with, and no other. So the first thing you have to do is accept that. Then, hopefully, with the benefit of advice and insights given throughout this book series, you can determine how to make the very best of it.

The key 'problem' traits

This book series has repeatedly touched on some key genetic – and often more autistic – 'mind' traits in Collies that may, if less well understood or managed, increase their chances of developing more challenging behaviours later on. This relates especially to their role as social companions.

The traits in question are:

1. Hypersensitivity to sensory stimuli.
2. Obsessive fixations on sensory stimuli.
3. Obsessive-compulsive patterns of behaviour, particularly in relation to moving things.
4. Greater fear or intolerance of the new.
5. Lower social awareness or recognition.
6. Control neuroses revolving round defence of personal space and resources.
7. Poor impulse control.
8. Higher levels of owner/human dependence.
9. Lower levels of human engagement.

Note that some of these traits can also bring advantages. For example, dogs with higher human dependency and higher sensory sensitivity are often easier to train and more responsive to training, as outlined in the next chapter.

Remember that it is not just the presence of these key traits that will be most significant in a dog, but how intensely they may feature in him, and how they may be expressed or directed. Remember, too, that the reason why Collies from purer 'working' breeding or backgrounds often have more of these traits is because of the genetic connection that exists in them between higher 'working' instinct and a generally more autistic canine mind.

Now let's see exactly how and why these specific traits in Collies can inspire more problematic behaviours in them later on.

1.   HYPERSENSITIVITY TO SENSORY STIMULI

Heightened sensory sensitivity – especially to noise, light, touch and movement – is commonly found in people on the autistic spectrum, and is also pretty common in Border Collies. The more extreme the sensory sensitivity in the dog, however, the more extreme his reactions to sensory stimuli may become.

People on the autistic spectrum often talk of having less of a mental 'filter' when it comes to the amount, and intensity, of sensory experience that crashes into their minds from their environment. This can sometimes be quite stressful or overwhelming.

Because a Collie's hearing is far more sensitive than a human's, we may not always appreciate how much physical pain, as well as mental pain, louder sounds may cause him. We also need to bear in mind that it is the memory of this physical pain that roots itself in the dog's sub-conscious mind, and

thereafter helps intensify so many noise-related phobias later on. In similar vein, some dogs will find moving objects – and especially noisy things that move – highly provocative on both a sensory and mental level. This means that once a dog has had this experience, he can really struggle not to mount some more immediate defensive, or offensive, response towards them.

To anyone who finds this reaction in any way abnormal, I would ask this simple question: how long can you tolerate a noisy fly buzzing constantly around you, and into your immediate head space, before you are filled with an overwhelming desire to swat it, or otherwise remove it from your presence, due to the level of mental and sensory provocation it is causing you? It is just that your own sensory settings may be set at a very different level to your dog's, in terms of what you feel least able to mentally tolerate, or most motivated to react to.

Mirroring the more unfiltered sensory input experienced by autistic people, I have frequently

Sensory flooding: Environments containing too much sensory input, in the way of sound, movement, light and crowding can overload the Collie's highly sensitive brain, and result in more fearful or reactive behaviour.

PHOTO: CAROL PRICE

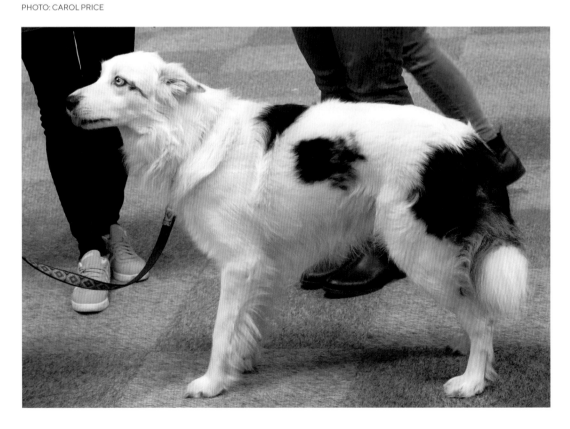

seen Collies entering virtual mental meltdown – i.e. cringing, cowering, shaking, panting, running or lunging – in the face of similar sensory overload or 'swamping' from their environment. Sights, smells, sounds, movement. There is just too much incoming sensory traffic for their brains to process all at once, especially in crowded, noisy places such as busy streets, with lots of loud oncoming motor traffic.

The dog's self-defence programming can also go haywire in the face of this sensory bombardment – he doesn't know whether to try to flee or lash out. Or sometimes he may just enter a state of total paralysis, and freeze to the spot, unable to move.

People often consider dogs like these to be more 'nervous' about the outside world, when they simply have a far more acute level of sensory awareness. This can be a quite physically unpleasant experience for them, as well as a mentally unpleasant one. Moreover, once the dog equates the outside world, beyond his home environment, with higher levels of sensory discomfort, or pain, then it is easier to understand his developing reluctance to face that outside world again.

There are few easy answers, or solutions, to dogs whose level of sensory awareness is too acute for the kind of modern life situations or environments they regularly find themselves in. The best we can do is develop a greater awareness of their struggles, try to desensitise them more to these challenges (see Chapter 8 on *Fear and its Fallout*) and better control the level of sensory assault they are exposed to on a daily basis (as outlined in Chapter 10 on *Sensory Detox*).

2. OBSESSIVE FIXATIONS ON SENSORY STIMULI

3. OBSESSIVE COMPULSIVE PATTERNS OF BEHAVIOUR *(particularly in relation to moving things)*

In Book One of this series, I highlighted how an obsession with sensory detail - such as the movement of lights or objects - plus a need to indulge in more compulsive and endlessly repetitive patterns of behaviour were both autistic traits. They are also key mental motivators of much of the working behaviour seen in sheepdogs. (i.e. continuous eyeing, chasing and herding).

However, if you remove dogs with these kinds of more obsessional and compulsive working patterns from livestock, they are often forced to find another target for them instead. This could be traffic, trains,

Sensory obsessions: Collies are renowned for their heightened reactivity to moving objects of any kind.

Fear of the new: Some Collies are more open to newer experiences, or encounters with those they know less well, others may react with far more apprehension or anxiety.

water, leaves, dust, lights and shadows –anything, in fact, that either moves or has the capacity to be made to move.

People who despair at this habit in Collies, or think it should be more easily stopped or eradicated, may not always understand the true force of the deeper compulsions driving the dog's behaviour, which act much like intense mental itches that constantly have to be scratched. This is because they are coming from the dog's more primal and instinctive brain, over which he has far less conscious control (far more on this phenomenon in Chapter 7: *The Instinctive and Impulsive Mind*.)

As outlined in Book Two, *Essential Life Skills and Learning*, it is crucial to identify dogs with these more obsessive-compulsive mental traits – when it comes to eyeing and chasing – as early on in life as possible. This is in order that these traits only get used or re-channelled in the most positive and healthy of ways, as opposed to getting progressively more and more out of your control.

4. GREATER FEAR OR INTOLERANCE OF THE NEW

The Collie's common dislike, or distrust, of newer or stranger things has already been covered in some detail in Books One and Two of this series,

as well as in Chapter 2 of this book on *The Collie Spectrum*. Essentially the dog sees any interruption in 'sameness' as potentially threatening, which thereafter explains some of his more anxious or fearful responses to it, in whatever form it may take.

The reason I keep stressing the need for owners to understand this trait, is so that they can better prepare for it when their dogs are younger, and at a stage in their lives when they are most amenable to having their social tolerance better shaped or stretched.

Moreover, different Collies may still deal with change very differently, according to how they are wired. Some may view 'change' or stranger things, for instance, as something that just momentarily unnerves them, after which they soon recover and adapt. These are the dogs in whom this 'newness aversion' trait is far less extreme, and thus far less likely to evolve into a bigger future problem.

Others may respond more violently. They may try to actively avoid or evade the stranger thing that unnerves them. Or they may freeze and refuse to move when invited or encouraged to confront it. Alternatively, in the case of stranger dogs or people, they may act more defensively, with aggression, in order to repel the sense of threat they represent in the dog's mind.

Once again it is important to understand that these fear or anxiety-based reactions are emanating from the dog's more primitive and instinctive sub-conscious mind, rather than reactions he consciously thinks about first. But dogs in whom such reactions are more extreme obviously have the capacity to develop bigger problems with their future behaviour. More on this subject in Chapter 8 on *Fear and its Fallout* and Chapter 9 on *Aggression*.

5. LOWER SOCIAL AWARENESS OR RECOGNITION

There are so many ways in which your Collie may be viewing, or reading, his external world differently to yourself. This is due to his rather different levels of sensory awareness and, often, a different type of social awareness.

I am not sure we always have the most accurate picture, as humans, of how our dogs perceive us as fellow beings. Or, indeed, how well, or not, they relate socially to all other animals or people they encounter.

Here is just one example of different levels of social awareness in a dog, which is apparent even at puppy stage. If a puppy bites your fingers and you yell, and he immediately stops, this is usually because he has sufficient social awareness to recognise that those fingers are attached to you as a fellow social being. If he stops biting when you yell, and then immediately looks at you to check your next response, this is all the more likely. In the same way he might immediately stop biting a fellow littermate when he makes the same sound. In other words, his level of social awareness can be linked to his level of bite inhibition.

Conversely, if a puppy bites your fingers and you yell and he does not stop, or look at you, or even intensifies his aggression still further, this may not be because he is 'nastier', or 'naughtier'. It is because he has poorer social awareness/recognition. He is seeing your fingers less as part of you, as a fellow social being, and more as quite separate 'objects' he has less inhibition about attacking, or even unleashing more predatory impulses upon.

This is just one example of the difference between dogs with higher or lower levels of social recognition or awareness. Sometimes dogs gradually develop better social awareness – and thus

Poorer social awareness, and a preference to remain more socially detached within their own little mental world, is commoner in Collies than many owners might realise.
PHOTO: CAROL PRICE

bite inhibition, too – as they get older, especially with the right guidance. But at other times greater social awareness, or recognition, becomes an on-going life problem for the dog.

When trying to understand the greater social capacity – or incapacity – of dogs, as well as any less favourable social reactions in them, it is a mistake to do so from the perspective of your own more normal and socially well-adjusted human brain. You have to see it, instead, within the limits of what any dog's more individual mind is capable of.

Autistics often talk about the way they try to mimic, or copy, what they imagine to be more 'normal' human social cues and reactions, because these things do not otherwise come naturally, or instinctively, to them. Often they will call this behaviour in themselves 'social masking'.

Some autistics have a kind of 'social blindness' that makes them not only unable to read the finer behavioural nuances of many human social contexts or interactions, but also to better distinguish between more threatening, or less threatening, social signals or approaches from others. Sometimes, also, they may not easily recognise people they have already met before. All these factors are what contribute to making social situations so stressful for them, or the source of such higher anxiety.

I think that a similar problem can apply in many Collies, in terms of their more general levels of social recognition and awareness. In some dogs it is very good, allowing the dog to appear more outwardly benign and confident in nature and have fewer problems in all his interactions with others, be they canine or human. In other dogs the social recognition/awareness levels are not so good. This means the dog struggles far more to understand, or relate to, a host of different social situations or interactions occurring around him. This, in turn, is what may inspire more fearful or defensive patterns of behaviour in him – a phenomenon I view in dogs as 'social panic'. It is what also gives the impression that the dog is rather more nervous or 'nasty' in nature.

So, if you experience issues like this with your own Collie, rule number one is to never assume that he is seeing any social situation as you are, whether this involves other people, or other dogs, or even yourself. What you see as a pretty benign social interaction may hold greater fears for him, as he is less able to read or understand it in the same way as you.

Over time, many Collies can greatly increase their levels of social competence and tolerance with the right training (of a kind outlined in Book Two of this series). This involves conditioning the dog to adopt set patterns of positive behaviour, in different social contexts, that prove consistently rewarding for him, and the owner taking far greater control of all their dog's social interactions.

If you feel that your dog's social fears or aggression levels are already more serious, there will be far more advice on this in Chapter 8 on *Fear and its Fallout* and Chapter 9 on *Aggression*.

6. CONTROL NEUROSES (revolving round defence of personal space and resources)

In Book One of this *Breed Apart* series, I outlined how many Collies may be driven by a desire to control not just the actions of others, but also their more immediate personal space. Traditionally this powerful instinct is thought to stem from the Collie's livestock working past, but more likely the instinct came first in the dog, and then later the working use it was put to.

With such an instinct, the key question then arises (as outlined in Chapter 2 *The Collie Spectrum*) as to whether the dog is more motivated to use psychological manipulation as a form of control – i.e. staring, whining, pawing, barking – which can be annoying enough. Or whether he is more motivated to use aggression instead.

Dogs that will more readily use aggression as a tool of control, are also more likely to attack their owners. This is especially true when placed in situations of greater confrontation, or when desiring to retain control over valuable resources. This could be food, bed area, or more strategic territorial areas such as the hallway, stairs, or front door. Their lower inhibition about using aggression, as well as the often less predictable nature of this behaviour in them, is what can make dogs like these so dangerous.

Control neuroses: Some Collies have a stronger need to protect personal space or more valuable resources — such as toys, food, territory or bedding — and may react more defensively whenever these suddenly appear under threat. It is a purely instinctive survival response in the dog, rather than one more consciously chosen.
PHOTO: CAROL PRICE

7. POOR IMPULSE CONTROL

Throughout this book series I constantly refer to the issue of 'impulse control' in Collies, in terms of what a critical factor it can be in determining how dogs will behave, or react in different situations, especially those producing greater mental pressure in the dog concerned.

Levels of mental impulse control in any of us are, in short, all that stand between our feelings or desires staying in our minds, or bursting out instead into physical reactions. There is always a very complex balance going on between the mind and body in terms of what thoughts or emotional sensations should, or should not, get translated into physical activity, as well as what that physical activity should be.

If you have good impulse control then it takes far more in the way of external provocation to trigger stronger physical reactions in you, such as aggression, excitement, terror or hysteria. You may also be less prone to addictive behaviours, or more

Impulse control: The all-important mental factor. How well your dog is able to control his physical responses to emotional sensations like fear, excitement or frustration will govern so many other aspects of his behaviour.

obsessive-compulsive patterns of activity. Whereas if you have far poorer levels of impulse control you are much more vulnerable to explosive physical reactions, which are far harder to consciously contain, or a range of more addictive and obsessive-compulsive habits which, again, may seem much harder to resist.

Once we understand this, we also better understand a lot of the differences that can occur in Collie personality and behaviour as a result of their own more individual levels of impulse control. Frequently this will have a genetic root. Collies from purer working backgrounds, for instance, often have poorer impulse control, because of a past need for them to have sharper and quicker responses to threat, or movement, when managing livestock.

Dogs may often be born with a propensity towards poorer or greater impulse control. But it is still possible to train and condition them to have greater impulse control, which otherwise may not come more naturally to them.

8. HIGHER LEVEL OF OWNER/ HUMAN DEPENDENCE

Collies can have a capacity to bond very strongly to the human(s) they live with, as one might expect of dogs who have been bred for generations to work with one master or handler. But sometimes this trait is misread. It is most commonly regarded as 'loyalty' which, to some extent, it may well be. But it is also about the dog's keen desire to preserve sameness in his life – which a more consistent human presence represents – and to cling on to the security of what is familiar.

It is in the nature of many Collies to make one most intense social bond in their lives which eclipses, in strength, the quality of any others they may make. Sometimes this bond may get attached to another dog, but more often than not it gets attached to an owner.

The upside of this stronger level of emotional/ psychological attachment is that it leads to dogs that are far more eager to please and thus easier to train. But the downside can be dogs who cope far less well when left alone; a subject covered more fully in Chapter 6 on *Separation Issues*.

9. LOWER LEVELS OF HUMAN ENGAGEMENT

Not all Collies will make the same kind of intense social bond with their human owners, and some dogs may appear rather more detached from them, and rather less willing – or able – to engage in more affectionate behaviour with them, or listen and respond more readily to anything they have to say.

Dogs like these can often be viewed as more 'stubborn', 'wilful' or 'disobedient' when, in fact, they often lack the higher level of social awareness – and psychological neediness – required to make stronger and more co-operative bonds with others. This, in turn, impacts on how responsive they may be to human desires or disapproval.

There will be more on dogs like these in the next chapter.

The link between traits and problems

Hopefully this chapter will make readers far more aware of the link that exists between certain mental traits in Collies, and the kind of behaviour issue – or psychological outlook – they may later inspire. For it can be common for owners to look everywhere else for the cause of such problems in their dogs, other than inside the basic inherited chemistry of their minds.

The more dependent, and independent, dog: Some Collies (top) become highly attached to their owners, psychologically, whereas others (bottom) will remain more detached. The latter type of dog may sometimes prove harder to train.

PHOTOS: CAROL PRICE

CHAPTER 5:

LESS RESPONSIVE DOGS

Why isn't your dog very 'obedient'?

Do not take your dog's 'obedience' for granted: A Collie's level of responsiveness towards your requests, or commands, may be linked to many deeper mental factors which you need to be aware of.
PHOTO: CAROL PRICE

Some Collies, without doubt, are not always as responsive, or trainable, as we would like them to be. It can often be frustrating to own dogs like these, especially given the breed's wider reputation for being more biddable in nature. So this chapter is going to focus on the commonest reasons why 'lower responsiveness' in Collies occurs, beginning once again with basic genetics.

If you have always known or owned very 'obedient' Collies, who are highly responsive to any command, and appear to hang on their owner's every word, you may have come to consider this the 'norm' for the breed.

But actually there can be types of Collie who are not always so responsive to owner commands, and can be harder to train or keep under more constant control. Dogs like these can be pretty bad for your blood pressure. But their origins – much like any other type of Collie – are likely to go some way back in the breed's history.

Those with particularly good memories may recall Herdman's Tommy, a dog I mentioned in Book One of this series, with regard to the modern Border Collie's earliest genetic origins. He was a significant dog in the breed, dating back to the early 1900s, and a grandson of the even more legendary founding dog, Old Hemp. Tommy had some plusses as a worker, and sired some subsequent International Supreme (trialling) Champions. However, as an individual he was also known for "not submitting well to discipline" and, as a trial competitor, often proved too difficult to control.

I often think of Tommy today, when I see exasperated Collie owners, screeching futilely at a dog hurtling purposefully towards the horizon, and not of a mind to return to them very soon. For Tommy was exactly the kind of more 'control resistant' Collie I have mentioned elsewhere. He may not have been the most ideal or trainable of sheepdogs, but his genes and inherent qualities – for better or worse – were perpetuated into future generations of Collies, only to re-emerge again in modern dogs.

People may often feel dismayed or even 'cheated' when they end up with more of a Tommy type of Collie, especially if they have always had highly responsive and compliant Collies before. However,

dogs of his ilk are always going to recur in the breed, and even have their admirers. For few Collies of this type do not have some other redeeming features, even if these can take a while to emerge. Plus dogs who are more independent thinkers are often also the best problem solvers.

Other factors

Of course it would be wrong to imagine that genetic aspects of character are always the sole reason why a Collie may be far less responsive to your commands. As outlined more fully in Book Two, and later in this chapter, it can also be down to the quality of the training the dog received earlier in his life, and how well this was tailored to his personality.

Either way, whenever we ask a dog to do something, and he fails to do it, there is always some deeper reason for this. Which is what we have to unearth, if we aspire to have a more responsive dog in the future.

What is 'disobedience' and 'obedience'?

First, however, it can help to have a better understanding of what 'disobedience' or 'obedience' really represent in a dog, as mental and behavioural phenomena. Or what drives any dog to behave more or less 'obediently' than another. We often do not think enough about this.

The term 'disobedient' is routinely used to describe dogs who persistently fail to comply with an owner's commands, requests or instructions of any kind. Commonly, there can also be a sense that this is down to some more conscious choice on the dog's part; i.e. he is just *deliberately* being more 'defiant' or 'stubborn'.

There are, however, quite a variety of reasons why dogs find themselves less able – as opposed to less willing – to co-operate with our commands or demands of them (see, *Dogs and the Science of Compliance*), which we have to be better aware of, if we are ever to get the best out of any Collie we own.

In contrast to 'disobedience' we will view 'obedience' in a dog – i.e. the dog responding readily to our every request – as a tremendous virtue. But really – much like 'disobedience' – it is just the more likely by-product of a particular type of canine mind.

Self-motivators: Some Collies are more independent workers who prefer to pursue their own agendas and solve their own problems. You may read this type of behaviour in them as more 'defiant', 'stubborn' or 'disobedient'.

Working with less responsive dogs

If you have a Collie that you feel is fundamentally less responsive to anything you ask him to do, then the first obvious question to ask is, how much training has he had? The world is full of dogs who are deemed anything from 'dumb' to 'defiant' by their owners when they simply haven't been properly trained. Instead they have been yelled at, or otherwise chastised, for getting something wrong, because no one took the trouble to teach them any better.

Alternatively your whole approach to your dog could be wrong, in that you are just too loud, hectoring, pressurising or otherwise 'physically noisy' in the way you address him. This is often in the belief that your dog should always know, or understand, more than he does. This can cause immense stress to more sensitive dogs, and make them mentally switch off, or try to escape your more oppressive presence. Also see, *How you create a switched off dog*.

So rule number one is to assume that your dog knows less, in terms of the training commands you wish him to respond to, than you think he does. And be a lot more patient, quiet and calm in your whole approach to him. More sensory sensitive Collies, in

DOGS AND THE SCIENCE OF COMPLIANCE

More or less 'obedient' – or responsive – dogs do not just occur through chance, or more expert training. Often they occur instead as a result of how their minds are pre-programmed to function. In order for a dog to be more 'obedient' in nature and behaviour, for example, he usually has to have most of these inherent mental qualities:

1. **Higher level of owner/human dependency:** The dog has much more invested, psychologically and emotionally, in pleasing people. This also gives him a greater mental reward. Dogs who are less owner/human dependent do not have the same psychological/emotional investment in people, or need to please them. Nor do they get the same mental reward from this.

Reliance and response: The more your dog has psychologically invested in you, the more your disapproval matters to him and will deter him from doing things that might invoke it.

PHOTO: CAROL PRICE

2. **Higher level of social awareness:** The dog understands not only that his owner is a fellow social being, but also one of great personal value to him as a resource and provider of all his life needs. It therefore matters far more to the dog to keep securing this individual's approval through promptly responding to their desires. His greater understanding of human moods and body language also makes it easier for him to both anticipate and tune into these desires most effectively.

3. **Higher ability to understand, interpret and mentally retain different training requests and commands given by an owner/handler:** Not all dogs will have this same kind of learning capacity.

4. **Higher ability to mentally process different types of sensory information at once:** When the dog is looking at – or being visually distracted by – something else, he can still hear you and respond to what you are saying to him. Or even when the dog is smelling something, he can still hear you and respond to what you are saying to him. The owner's verbal (or visual) commands, in short, take priority in the dog's mind over any other competing sensory distractions in his environment. *Though note, this capacity/ability – as covered in Book Two – can also be greatly enhanced with the right training.*

5. **Higher levels of owner focus:** The dog develops the habit of more constant visual focus on his owner, meaning he is less likely to miss the next instruction he is given. (*Note again, as outlined in Book Two, you can greatly enhance this 'habit' with the right training*).

6. **Lower need for the dog to retain personal control over his own actions, movements and space and greater willingness to surrender control of these things to others.**

Exactly how these different traits – or lack of them – may affect your own dog's level of responsiveness is explained in greater detail in the main text of this chapter.

general, need to be addressed with the slowest and calmest of body language, and the most quiet and gentle of voice tones.

If, on the other hand, you have an essentially more 'control resistant' dog, he could find such heavier approaches far more personally threatening or confrontational. This could lead to a situation where the more you try to coerce him into doing anything, the more he will resist on principle, until you give up.

Improving your training

Everything you need to know about training Collies, and training different dogs in different ways, appears in Book Two of this series, which also gives extensive advice on what to do when your training goes wrong. Thus if you feel that most of your dog's perceived 'disobedience' problem could be purely down to a lack of the right training, this would be a good place to start.

It is also important not to feel daunted by the whole process of dog training, as so many owners can be, especially if they are relatively new to it. Just start with smaller goals or exercises that are of highest priority to you, and then work on from there. Also never compare yourself and your dog's progress to any other owner, or any other dog. You and your dog are totally unique as a partnership. And every human/dog partnership gets to where it needs to be in its own time, and in its own way.

Earlier in this chapter – and in the panel, *Dogs and the science of compliance* – I highlighted key mental factors that often make the biggest difference to how responsive your Collie may be to training or commands of any kind. Now I am going to explain, in greater depth, exactly how and why they can result in such different attitudes or reactions in dogs.

HOW YOU CREATE A SWITCHED OFF DOG

Owners are often not aware of the part they have played in creating a fundamentally less responsive dog, or one who noticeably switches off mentally whenever they ask him to do something.

This process can begin with something as simple as a wrong early training approach; i.e. coming suddenly into your dog's space, and being more pressurising or louder in your body language and voice tone. Or showing more obvious impatience and disapproval when your dog fails to understand what is desired of him, or gets something wrong. Such actions may seem pretty insignificant to you, but will have far more of a damaging impact on a highly sensitive dog. He may then equate any subsequent training approach from you with a more negative and worrying experience, which he will attempt to evade through mentally switching off.

Alternatively, some Collies react more adversely to the whole process of being more actively forced or pressurised into doing things. And once you have equated the training process in the minds of dogs like these with more worrying losses of personal control, you can then begin building a progressively more command-resistant and 'switched off' dog. Dogs like these always need to be *invited* to do things, in a way that does not invade their own space, and then find these actions intensely rewarding. They then later choose, by themselves, to do the same things, when you invite them to. Which is how they retain a greater sense of control and you still get the responses you require.

As it is not always easy to see ourselves as our dog sees us, during the training process, it can often be a good idea to get someone to film you training your dog. Then play it back, paying specific attention to the immediate effect of your different voice tones, actions or approaches on your dog's reactions or body language. Such exercises can be highly enlightening.

Gaining greater co-operation: If you control something that matters most to your dog — like a favourite toy — and also his access to it, you can use this to build ever higher levels of attention and response in him, even in dogs who are not natural 'people pleasers'.

The owner dependency factor

You may recall that the first higher 'obedience', or responsiveness, pre-requisite I outlined in dogs was greater owner dependency. The more dogs have invested, both psychologically and emotionally, in people, the more it matters for them to please them, or continually gain and retain their approval. Thus higher responsiveness emerges as a more natural instinct in them, as a result of this trait.

Conversely, dogs who do not have this same level of psychological dependency do not have the same kind of higher responsiveness instinct, either. That is, human approval gives them far less of a mental reward and, thus, is less of a motivator for their actions or behavioural choices. Similarly human disapproval acts as less of a deterrent, or inhibiting factor, for them, when it comes to their actions or behavioural choices.

So if you are basing your whole training and management of a dog like this on the premise that he should just *naturally* want to please you, or co-operate with you, you are heading down a pretty doomed path, in constantly trying to appeal to something that mentally isn't there.

A better approach would be to acknowledge first that your dog does not get that great a mental reward from the act of pleasing you. This may be frustrating, or even a bit hurtful, but it is also an inescapable reality. It means, too, that you will need to find other things – such as toys, games or food – from which he can get a far bigger mental reward and use these far more consistently in all your training, or interactions, with him if you want to keep securing higher levels of co-operation.

What matters most is that you keep connecting acts of co-operation in your dog with adequate mental rewards for him, so that such co-operation becomes far more of a chosen habit in him. Moreover, if you consistently *praise* your dog immediately before giving him any kind of physical reward – like a toy or food – eventually he will learn to associate your praise with the physical reward to come. This means your praise, in itself, can later become a reward for the dog – even in dogs who are not natural 'people pleasers' – because of what he mentally associates it with.

You will also need to understand that you being less 'happy' with your dog's behaviour will not unduly upset or inhibit him, in the way it might a more psychologically dependent dog. So you will have to rely on other strategies to stop him doing things you do not want him to do, or just better control what he does.

Key among these will be 'distraction' techniques, where you abort any less desirable actions or reactions in your dog via offering him a sufficiently high reward (i.e. food, toy, whatever works best) to do something more desirable instead, such as *sit*, or lie *down* and *watch* you (all covered in Book Two). This will also involve learning to read your dog's behaviour far more effectively, in terms of better anticipating what he is about to do, in order to prevent it. It will also improve your timing, given how rapidly some Collies will think and then react. Too often owners will only try to get their dog's attention back to them, with the use of rewards, long after the dog has already mentally committed himself to another course of action.

The social awareness factor

As outlined previously in this chapter, levels of social awareness in a dog can also be directly linked to his levels of responsiveness in training. The higher the dog's level of social awareness and ability, the more responsive he often is towards his owner, and the more skilled he becomes at both reading and anticipating his owner's desires. He is also able to build a far stronger social bond, in general, with his owner, which – for many dogs – results in greater responsiveness.

Most people only realise that their Collie has lower social awareness when they compare his behaviour to other Collies they have known who had far higher levels of social awareness and ability. Such differences may include the dog generally being less actively engaged with them, – that is, not constantly wanting to be with them, or do things with them. Or being far less obviously affected by any changes in an owner's behaviour, body language or mood, other than when it comes across as potentially threatening to them.

Dogs like these may be far happier to remain in their own little mental world, where they may pursue any number of more obsessive-compulsive hobbies, oblivious to the wider social arena around them. They will also be fundamentally less socially adaptive, unable to establish basic social connection with dogs or people they have just met, or know less well. They may see them in a more threatening light or just view them with complete indifference.

If you feel that you have a Collie like this, the first thing to do is recognise it, and then adapt your expectations of him accordingly. Your dog cannot help the greater social limitations of his brain, or change them, no matter how much you might want him to. However, you can begin working more effectively with his particular kind of mind.

First, as with less human dependent dogs, you have to identify the thing(s) in life that gives him the highest level of mental reward. It may be sensory fixating, i.e. continually eyeing some moving object or target. Or it may be food. Or it may be chasing a favourite toy. If your dog has developed a sensory fixation on something you cannot actively control yourself – such as shadows, or water, or dust or leaves – you must do your best to change this, and switch his more obsessive impulses on to something you can control instead, i.e. a toy. (Note: advice on this process was covered in Book Two of this series).

The most important thing of all is that you retain total control of what gives your dog the highest mental reward, and also control his access to it. Only then can you start more actively bargaining with him to get ever better responses from him, and habits of co-operation. Once you have got the thing he desires most in all the world, you have also got his attention, plus higher motivation to do what has to be done in order to secure what he wants. This includes better responding to your commands. Be aware, also, that there is nothing even vaguely socially demanding in this interchange for your dog. You are simply appealing to his innate sense of logic, in terms of what he has to do to get what he most desires.

Unfortunately, many owners with less socially aware Collies do not understand the need to continually bargain with their dogs in this way. This is not just to better secure and hold their co-operation, on a daily basis, but also as a substitute for having a more effective social and emotional bond with the dog concerned. An owner may try, instead, to exert more psychological pressure on the dog in order to appeal to feelings such as gratitude, respect or a sense of obligation that they believe should exist in their dog's mind, but don't.

Another commonly adopted option is to allow dogs free access, 24/7, to everything in life that gives them the highest mental buzz. Owners then find themselves with nothing to bargain with, when the dog becomes less responsive towards them.

The higher or lower trainability factor

Sometimes the worst thing that can happen to an owner is to have one Collie, or succession of Collies, with exceptionally high trainability in terms of the dog's ability to both learn, and retain, different training commands or exercises. Thereafter, any Collie they get with far lower abilities on this front, will come as a relative shock or disappointment to them, or be judged more harshly by comparison as being dumb or 'disobedient'.

It is important to understand that the trait of higher learning and training ability is not universally present in Collies. It is something you have to deliberately breed into them, or perpetuate through the right choice of breeding stock. Also, parent dogs who may have higher training/learning capacities themselves can still produce dogs in a litter who are not like this, due to a variety of ways in which different genes may be inherited and/or expressed in dogs.

Frequently owners will end up with more trainable Collies through sheer luck, rather than deliberate design. However, a more reliable way to get a Collie with high learning/training capacity is to get one from parents – or breeding lines – with this trait, and also better evaluate their puppies, to see which ones have inherited it.

Puppies with inherently higher learning/training ability are not that hard to spot. You can teach a pup of this type a most basic command – a *sit* or *down* – in return for rewards and he will not only master it in super-quick time but also remember it for longer. An hour, or even a day, after you first taught him that command, he will still remember what it means and how to respond to it. Whereas puppies with lower learning powers will not, or may need more consistent reminding or practice.

Faster and slower learners: Not all Collies can mentally retain what you teach them at the same speed, and may require greater time, patience and understanding to master more reliable responses.

Again, this is not the fault of the dog concerned. It is just the way he is wired. It also does not mean that he cannot be an utterly charming dog in other ways. Not all of us could master French or Quantum physics, for that matter, over a relatively short period of time, and then retain what we learned forever more. But it doesn't necessarily make us fundamentally worthless as human beings. Dogs with lower learning/training capacity need more patience, and greater recognition of their mental limitations, rather than owners who just keep jumping up and down with frustration and stressing them out.

The mental and sensory processing factor

Previously in this chapter I have outlined that a key factor in the higher responsiveness of Collies lies in the way they mentally process sensory information. I explained how information from a particular sense – for example, sight, hearing or smell – often shares the same brain space, meaning that dogs commonly have to mentally prioritise information from one sense over another. This, in turn, influences their later reactions.

With some dogs, sight information may take priority in the brain over hearing. This means that when a dog is visually occupied by something, he will be far less able to hear things around him, including your commands. With other dogs it will be smell, or scent, meaning that when the dog is smelling something more intently, he will also be less able to hear you.

Again people often read this behaviour as 'disobedience' when it is simply down to the sheer limits of any dog's brain, and powers of sensory processing. The Border Collie, however, often has a unique brain in this regard, in terms of his ability to process both sight and sound information almost simultaneously. This, in turn, is what allows the dog to both absorb and respond to a shepherd's verbal commands, or whistle, even while he is visually focused on sheep. Or follow an agility handler's

Seeing yourself as your dogs do: The author and her dogs. Sometimes it can really help to get someone to film you interacting or working with your dogs to see what you could be doing better.
PHOTO: JUDI ASBURY

Demand avoidance: A Collie with higher sensitivity to mental pressure, and loss of personal control, may struggle with exercises, like recall, or down and stay, where you appear to be overtly imposing your will on him, and so he may try to evade complying with such demands in any number of ways. It is a purely instinctive response in the dogs concerned, as opposed to any more imagined 'defiance' on their part, and they may require a far more enlightened approach to their training.

PHOTO: CAROL PRICE

verbal commands, while he is focused on the obstacles ahead.

This ability is too often taken for granted in Collies, with owners only tending to pay attention to it when it is noticeably absent. This usually results in a dog that cannot hear you while he is also visually fixated on something else – behaviour which you may read as him simply ignoring you.

Although some dogs will be more natural absorbers and processors of both sight and sound information at once, many Collies can also have this capacity enhanced in them with the kind of training outlined in Book Two of this series (Chapter 10). Thereafter you may find yourself with a rather more responsive dog, especially at greater distances away from you.

The owner focus factor

With or without higher mental processing skills, or learning ability, there is always a direct correlation in a Collie between the level of focus you are able to obtain, and retain, in him, and the level of his overall responsiveness to your commands. Until you are able to readily secure, and hold, your dog's attention in this way, you are unable to teach him much else – or maintain a greater control, in general, over his behaviour. You will spend your time instead more futilely talking to the back of his head.

In Book Two of this series, I outlined at length not only how vital the quality of *focus* is in Collies,

How essentially 'obedient' and responsive — or not — a Collie becomes in later life is not just down to chance. It also revolves around a number of individual mental factors in them, as well as more personally tailored training.

PHOTO: CAROL PRICE

but also how you could best teach and enhance this ability to make them infinitely more responsive to any other commands you might give them. So if you feel that your own dog's *focus* levels could be greatly improved, it is worth revisiting Book Two to brush up on them.

The control resistance factor

In our wider look at all the factors that might make one Collie more or less responsive to training, or commands, than another, we are finally going to look at the issue of control. If you have a fundamentally more control resistant Collie, there are always going to be commands he will have more difficulty with.

Typical examples are commands that attempt to place greater restriction over his actions or movements, such as *wait, stay, down* or *recall*. The more controlling the dog is, the less he likes to be controlled himself. By contrast, dogs who have less concern about surrendering personal control over their actions and movements find them far easier to comply with. This is especially the case if they have already been trained to find such compliance inherently non-threatening and also highly rewarding.

Many control resistant dogs can find themselves in much more of a mental quandary with these tasks. Part of them may want to comply with a command to do them, in order to take the owner's mental pressure off them, but the other part of their brain urges them to resist complying at all costs, for fear of the loss of control this represents.

Moreover, the longer the dog resists, the harder it can be for him to give up on this strategy, having already mentally invested so much in it. It can also be the reason why a non-recalling dog will hold out for so long before coming back to you; forever stalling, or delaying, the moment when his freedom, and personal control, is lost again.

Where owners go wrong in such situations is in imagining that this sort of 'hold out' behaviour is a sign of more conscious defiance in a dog, or some kind of calculated assault on their authority. It is a far more instinctive impulse, driven by the dog's deeper inherent terror of losing control.

It is vital to view the psychology of the control resistant dog in a more enlightened way if you are ever to improve your future responses from him.

What to do

As previously highlighted in *How you create a switched off dog (page 52),* sometimes with more control resistant dogs, it is not the training command or instruction they have greatest problems with, but the level of mental pressure or coercion they have come to associate it with. Therefore it is worth thinking harder about the manner in which you previously taught – or attempted to teach – your dog commands like *sit, down, wait, stay* and *recall,* if you are having problems with his responses to them. Then consider how they might be better, or more effective.

In Book Two of this series, I highlighted not just ways in which Collies can be best taught different commands – including *sit, down, wait, stay, recall* – but also how to adapt your training approach to your dog's more individual personality. This included dogs who are more control resistant in nature. For once you can better tune in to where your dog is mentally coming from, you are already on the way to better training results.

Mental differences

Hopefully, this chapter has made you aware that both 'obedience' and 'disobedience' – or higher or lower levels of responsiveness towards commands – are not always such simple reactions in dogs and can instead involve some more complex mental factors. Neither are they reactions, or behaviours, that dogs always consciously choose to adopt, and tend to originate instead from more inherent and instinctive aspects of the dog's mind.

Just better understanding this kind of reality also makes it easier for us to understand the mind of the less responsive dog, and the problems he may experience in better living up to what you desire of him.

If your dog is persistently 'non-co-operative' to your commands, another possibility to consider is that he is either deaf, or has some hearing defect, which would be worth checking out. However obvious this may seem, many owners can overlook it. Alternatively, a Collie may have some visual impairment which makes it harder for him to interpret any physical training gestures you may give him, especially from further away. It is yet another reason – as outlined in Book Two – why I always prefer to combine both physical hand and arm gestures and verbal cues for teaching different exercises to Collies.

CHAPTER 6:

SEPARATION ISSUES

Why can't your dog cope when you leave him?

Solitary stress: Separation issues in Collies can be complex, rooted both in the way we own dogs today, and the way we have evolved over time.
PHOTO: CAROL PRICE

At the beginning of the last chapter, I cited greater human dependency in dogs as a factor that usually made them easier to train. I also made the point that that this characteristic can have a downside, in terms of how less well the same kind of dogs cope when separated from their owners, or left alone by them at home.

Other than just excessive psychological dependence, there are in fact quite a number of reasons why Collies may find the experience of being separated from owners, or left alone by them, a more distressing experience. And as the wider phenomenon of 'separation trauma' in dogs is not always sufficiently understood, I am going to cover it more fully in this chapter.

A common problem

Separation trauma is one of the commonest behaviour problems – or reactions – seen in dogs today, as people lead ever busier lives, and have to leave their dogs for longer periods on their own at home. The dogs may then react very adversely to this experience, i.e. barking, whining or howling non-stop, or losing toilet control, or trashing various fixtures and fittings in the home to release stress and anxiety.

Owners, understandably, can find this kind of reaction in their dogs quite distressing. They may also seek to 'cure' their separation trauma with sedation medication, as if it were a type of illness best controlled this way. In reality it is a more predictable psychological reaction, given the nature of the circumstances the dog finds himself in: i.e. abandoned, alone, confined, helpless and deprived of the most valuable resource in his life – his owner(s).

With canine separation trauma, in essence, we come face to face with two modern species' needs in constant conflict with each other. The first is the owner's need to spend periods away from their dog, be this for personal or professional reasons. And the other is the dog's need to have an owner's presence more consistently around him, in order to preserve his sense of security and optimum psychological health. Thereafter it is in the on-going clashing of these different needs that produces all the problems for both dogs and their owners.

The dependent dog

People do not always understand how or why dogs become so psychologically dependent and reliant on them, and their presence. However, this characteristic in modern dogs has not arisen by chance. Instead it dates back to the whole way we have genetically evolved dogs, over time, to be more biddable companions.

Our earlier ancestors began the process through deliberately favouring dogs to keep, and breed from, that retained and sustained a state of arrested development. In other words they remained more 'puppyish' in nature throughout their lives. Through being infinitely more playful, babyish, helpless, malleable and eager to please, this made them far more endearing and appealing to us as social companions, and also a lot easier to handle and control. In contrast, dogs who went on to assume more adult and independent identities tended to pose a greater challenge.

The genetic tendency, in modern dogs, towards greater psychological dependency gets further adapted and intensified by their upbringings. In that they mostly project their dependency on to humans as young puppies, because it is humans who assume the 'parent dog' role so early in their lives; providing them with every life resource they will ever need, without them ever having to hunt or work for them.

Alone and nowhere to go: It is not just an owner's absence that can cause dogs great distress, but also the state of confinement they tend to be left in when the owner departs.
PHOTO: CAROL PRICE

Thus there is progressively less motivation for dogs to ever really grow up mentally, and establish far more independent ways of thinking and behaving.

This is the opposite of what happens in the wild where, beyond a certain age, dogs need to not only carry their own weight in a pack, or family group, but also develop their own more self-reliant adult identities and behaviours. Alternatively, they may need to leave their original group and either lead a totally independent existence, or join/begin a new one elsewhere.

Helplessness

Similarly, the more intense anxiety many adult domestic dogs may experience, and display, when an owner leaves them alone at home – with symptoms that typically include pacing, whining, barking and howling – are not replicated in wild dogs, when separated from others, once they have attained maturity. They are far more reminiscent of the kind of acute distress you will see in young puppies when separated from their mothers.

So what happens, in essence, is that we breed and condition dogs to retain a more infantile and human-dependent mind-set, which holds benefits for us in many ways. But it can also be what then prompts them to collapse into a state of total mental helplessness when we leave them.

A dog's individual level of owner – and human – dependency is thus usually some significant guide to how well he may cope mentally when he is separated from that owner, and left alone at home. But it is not the only factor, by any means.

The stress of confinement

This is because another key – and often more underestimated – component in canine separation trauma is the relative state of confinement that most dogs are left in once owners depart.

Thus, over and above any human dependency issues, dogs whose mental health is more dependent on them feeling a sense of control over their own actions and movements will always cope less well with this predicament. They may also be

Waiting for you: For most dogs, the front door marks the point at which the owner was last seen before departing, and thus where they will often remain rooted in anticipation of their return.
PHOTO: CAROL PRICE

the same dogs you will find tearing at flooring, doors, or doorway frames with their teeth and claws, when owners leave them confined, in a frenzied attempt to escape. Or chewing and clawing the inside of their crates if they have been unlucky enough to be left in one for longer periods of time.

This is utterly desperate behaviour on the part of any dog. I am often aghast at owners whose dogs behave this way when they leave them, yet still do not acknowledge that this is a *big problem*, which needs some more immediate addressing.

Loss of sameness

As mentioned in past chapters, there is another element to separation trauma that is not always considered, especially in more autistic dogs. This is the dog's inability to cope with the sudden withdrawal of 'sameness', in the form of his owner leaving him.

The owner's on-going presence, in short, plays a significant part in maintaining the dog's mental equilibrium and sense of security. Dogs with this kind of mental outlook will often stay right by the front door when an owner is out and never move from it, clinging to the point where 'sameness' was last seen, before an owner departed, and where they also desperately hope it will return again. Sometimes they will turn their anxiety about 'loss of sameness' more inwards and at others become far more vocal and physically distressed.

Crisis and relief of crisis

Owners may often mistake a dog who is euphoric with relief when they return with one who just "always gives them a lovely greeting".

You know that moment when you come home, and you think your dog is going crazy with joy to see you, just because he loves you so deeply and missed you so much? Well just as likely this is a display, instead, of his total and utter relief that the human life support is back again, and the state of confinement ended. For dogs soon work out that when they are left confined, they need a human to release them from the state of confinement again.

Most dogs become human dependent, specifically, as opposed to just dependent on the presence of another social being in their lives, such

as another dog. This is an important difference to establish, as many owners can seek to solve their dog's separation trauma problems through getting him another dog 'for company'. They do this out of the misconception that he is simply 'lonely' when they leave him, as opposed to panic stricken by the combined psychological hits of enforced confinement, plus the loss of sameness in the form of his most valuable life resource. Dogs may not readily be consoled by the presence of other dogs in such circumstances, and may even pass their own separation trauma symptoms on to them.

The tendency for dogs to be mostly human dependent, as opposed to just 'company' dependent, also explains why they always cope better when left in the presence of another human minder, in their owner's absence, even if they do not know the minder that well.

The nature of our relationship with dogs

The reason separation trauma – or separation panic, as I often view it – can sometimes be so hard to resolve in individual dogs, is because we cannot isolate this problem from the deeper rooted issues lying behind it. By this I mean the nature of the dogs we have evolved today, and the nature of the relationships we establish and reinforce on a daily basis from their earliest puppyhood, and social development, onwards.

Pretty commonly, it is one where we encourage their reliance and dependency when it suits or benefits us, but cannot equip them to cope better when our presence is suddenly removed – especially for longer or more unpredictable periods of time.

We do not do this with any sense of unkind intent, but because we genuinely do not understand how our dogs got to be – and feel – so helpless without us. Or because we think that the more we leave our dogs on their own, the better they will eventually cope with it, when the reverse is often true.

The separation issue is also further complicated by fundamental differences in the way human and canine brains work, or regard a specific life event. For example, in order to better 'reassure' them, owners want their dogs to understand the following things:

- That they have to leave them alone sometimes for specific reasons.
- That when they leave them they will not be gone for long, or …
- That whenever they leave them they will always be coming back again.

However, while the human brain can master these more abstract concepts of time and movement, which project into the future, the canine brain cannot. So each time a dog is left, he cannot conjure up a concept in his mind of when, or if, you may return. He can only refer mentally to how he felt the last time he was placed in this particular separation 'picture' or situation. This could be anything from mildly uneasy to all out hysterical, depending on the dog concerned, and what his past life experiences may have been.

It is so important to grasp the difference between human thinking and canine thinking in these situations, and not judge your dog, or his behaviour, as if he were – or should be – capable of thinking more like you do.

Obvious and less obvious stress

The true level of distress any dog experiences when left alone, cannot be gauged solely by external symptoms such as barking, howling, whining, destructiveness or fouling. A lack of such overt symptoms could lead owners to imagine that their dog is 'coping fine' with being left alone when he really isn't on a deeper level.

For several past studies have revealed that dogs who display more extreme physical reactions to being left, and those who don't, often have exactly the same heightened levels of cortisol (stress hormone) in their bodies. It's just that some dogs turn their stress symptoms more inwardly, which is definitely not the same as 'coping'.

Moreover, dogs who display more violent physical reactions to being left often do so through having poorer impulse control in general; i.e. a lower ability to stop thoughts or emotions exploding into physical reactions. Dogs with higher impulse control could be suffering just as much inside, only without more actively expressing it.

SEPARATION DISTRESS:
How you push the panic button for your dog

One of the biggest mistakes owners can make – with the best of intentions – is to repeatedly give their dogs set, and more obvious, cues that they are about to leave them for some time.

In other words, each time you depart you will say the same thing to your dog; like you won't be long, or that he has got to be good etc., and/ or give him a treat. These words or measures are simply to make you feel better about leaving your dog. In reality they offer no comfort to him whatsoever, and instead can have quite the opposite effect in immediately signalling to him that he is about to be left alone for some time, because you always do and say these same things just before leaving him.

Thus, inadvertently, you have just pushed

the panic button in your dog's head. And that is why he often will not eat the treat you leave for him *because it is immediately connected to you going*. He may well only eat it when you come back and his stress levels go back down again.

It is always best to say absolutely nothing to your dog when you leave, and depart in the kind of abrupt and casual manner you would adopt if you were just popping out for a few seconds to get something from the car.

Also be aware that things like locking up, getting your keys and phone or putting on certain shoes or a particular coat also alerts your dog to the fact that you will be leaving the home. So it's a good idea to regularly go through these same short rituals daily *without* leaving, until your dog shows zero anxiety when you do this, and remains settled and relaxed. Also see, *Making separation more bearable*, a bit later.

Can separation anxiety be cured?

The more we appreciate the deeper psychological – and evolutionary – issues involved in much canine separation anxiety, the more we may distrust behaviourists who claim that all dogs with these kinds of problem can be cured. I certainly do not believe this is true.

I think it depends greatly on the nature of the dog concerned, i.e. how much his brain leads him towards feelings of panic or helplessness when left alone, how physically reactive he is when panicked, and how long, and how often, he is allowed to keep repeating and reinforcing high anxiety behaviours when his owner is out – to the point where they become a deeply ingrained habit.

It is often just the *symptoms* of separation anxiety – like barking, howling and destructiveness – that owners mostly preoccupy themselves with as opposed to the state of mind that triggers all this behaviour.

They may, as a result, decide to put their dogs in crates or cages to stop them being destructive when left. Or decide to place some 'anti-barking' device on them, which makes barking far less pleasant for them. However, they still haven't solved the problem of a dog who remains as anxious as ever, when left, and then finds himself with even fewer physical outlets on which he can displace the stress this induces in him. And, rest assured, that stress will always need to go somewhere.

Much the same can apply to tranquiliser or sedative medications for dogs with separation anxiety issues. Tempting though they be for those whose dog's problems are more acute, still all they do is subdue the symptoms of separation trauma in a dog, as opposed to tackle its true cause – the dog's inability to cope without a human presence, plus the additional stress of confinement.

Making separation more bearable

Arguably there is one sure-fire way to prevent your dog ever having separation issues – and that's don't leave him alone! And if you are an owner who can always be there for your dog, he is fortunate. Though that said, human attention can become just too powerful a drug for some dogs, in that the more they get, the more they will expect and the more they will want and demand on a regular basis.

For the majority of us, however, a 24/7 owner presence is less realistic to achieve. But I do believe there are compromises and adjustments that can be made in order that dogs are able to cope better with the experience of being left alone. These are:

1. TIME OUTS

It is best never to give your dog the expectation, early in life, that he has the right to have access to you 24/7, wherever you go. It may be flattering to you, but it is simply not healthy to have a dog who feels compelled to shadow your movements constantly, like a personal stalker. And it is even less healthy to encourage this. The more you build this expectation of 'constant access' in your dog, the worse he will cope when you have to leave him.

Instead, get your dog into the habit of having regular separation periods away from you, of an hour or more at a time, initially while you are at home, and using a dog gate to separate him, if necessary. At first your dog may protest and whine about this, but you *must* ignore him totally until he settles down quietly again. And only ever reunite with your dog *while he remains quiet and settled*, otherwise you will be constantly rewarding him for more distressed and agitated behaviour.

Sometimes it can help to place a symbolic object – such as a chair, an ornament, or even a radio with the volume turned low – in front of the dog gate to indicate to your dog that he is about to have a period of separation from you, which will only end once he is quiet and settled. Always remember to remove the object when you reunite with your dog. *And never end the separation from your dog until he is quiet and settled again.*

If your dog successfully understands that this object means he must settle quietly on his own for a while, you can then eventually put the same object in front of the gate before you actually leave the home. But you may need to build up the amount of time you leave him like this more gradually, in line with his ability to cope.

It is also a good idea to make your dog sleep somewhere that is separate from you – e.g. downstairs – at night. Once again, although *you* may like him sleeping in your bedroom or on your bed, it is in no way helping him to build up a greater ability to cope with periods on his own.

2. NEGATIVE CUEING

Avoid any kind of *more negative cueing* before you leave your dog. (See *Separation distress: How you push the panic button for your dog*.)

3. MAINTAINING ROUTINE

Try to make any separation periods *as routine as possible*. Dogs always cope better when periods of separation are more routine, or become more predictable. So if you have certain tasks to do away from home that are time flexible, try to schedule them in around the same time of day so that your dog will always be more prepared to be left.

4. DAMAGE LIMITATION

Do not leave your dog alone for longer or less predictable periods of time, as these can do the real damage, psychologically. The most I would ever recommend leaving a dog for – and even then with some reluctance – is two hours, and any more than that I would get a minder to be with my dogs. Similarly I will get a minder or sitter if I am going to leave my dogs at less usual times, or for a less predictable amount of time.

Ideally you should try to build up a network of other dog owning friends, so that you can all take turns to look in on, or after, each other's dogs when needed. In the modern age of social networking such arrangements have become increasingly easy to set up.

When is too long?

People can get very heated over the issue of how long you should leave a dog alone for, with most of the 'upper' periods debated – like my own two hours – being entirely arbitrary, as opposed to more effectively or accurately tailored to the separation tolerance of the dog concerned.

Similarly there are people who consider it acceptable to leave a dog at home alone all day while they go to work. I believe it is unacceptable, not just for reasons already outlined, but because dogs cannot be highly emotionally intelligent beings when it suits us to imagine this, and far less emotionally intelligent beings when it doesn't.

A recent study, for example, has revealed that dogs – and I am pretty sure Border Collies! – can possess intelligence on a par with a two-year-old human toddler. I do not know anyone who would think it acceptable to leave their two-year-old toddler locked in a cage, or their kitchen, all day while they went to work, let alone one who would then expect to come back to a pristine home and a thoroughly calm and happy little individual with no mental issues. But I know a fair few people who expect this of dogs.

There can also be a sizeable element of 'out of sight, out of mind' involved when dogs are left more lengthily alone. In the sense that, as long as you are not physically witnessing the distress your dog experiences when you are not there, it is not really happening. But actually it is.

Ultimately we live in an imperfect world, where none of us ever does everything right all the time when it comes to dogs. But there's still no escaping the reality that dogs who are left alone more often, and particularly for longer and more predictable periods of time, will always carry more stress throughout their lives than those who are not. This is because of the way they are mentally designed, and because of the way we own them. And this, in turn, may have some deeper impact later on their mental and physical wellbeing.

This is why good breeders and rescue centres always want to know how long you would intend to leave a dog alone for, before they let you have him. They know how much this matters – and why.

CHAPTER 7:

THE INSTINCTIVE AND IMPULSIVE MIND

Understanding more sub-conscious thinking and behaviours in your dog

Of all the misconceptions that commonly exist about dogs, one of the greatest is that they can always consciously control what they do – when they can't. Anymore than people can always consciously control what they do.

The truth lies elsewhere in that more primal and powerful part of any animal's brain which comprises the sub-conscious mind.It is the home of all memories, instincts, impulses and emotions, and all the deeper survival programming designed to keep us alive.

In many animals, this primitive and instinctive kind of thinking is now thought to drive behaviour more forcefully than we may have ever considered before. It may also be the reason why some dog behaviours seem so much more resistant to being changed than others – including a number of behaviours seen in the Border Collie – unless we can better understand and address our dog's more primal inner programming.

Thus, this chapter is going to explore the differences between more conscious and sub-conscious thinking and behaving in dogs, and Border Collies in particular. Not least because better recognising the part your dog's sub-conscious mind plays in so much of his behaviour can also help you to become a far more insightful owner and handler.

The effects of sub-conscious thinking on behaviour

Over my years of working with problem dogs – and Collies in particular – an issue that long intrigued me was why some dogs were better able to change their more compulsive or challenging behaviours than others, especially on a longer lasting basis. Then I realised it was chiefly down to two basic factors. Firstly, how amenable their sub-conscious minds were to the prospect of different thinking, particularly in terms of what was, and was not, threatening. Secondly, how well a dog was able to

Sub-conscious 'flooding': Dogs with weaker training — including that involving better focus and impulse control — will always struggle harder to resist the pull of other surrounding distractions.

exert better control over his inner mental impulses, and avoid them being translated into physical reactions. For the latter is one of the commonest perpetuators of both aggressive and obsessive-compulsive behaviour problems in Border Collies.

Moreover, because the sub-conscious or 'survival' mind holds such influence over a dog's behaviour, until this deeper mental powerhouse in him can be convinced that changes in thinking or acting are necessary, the dog cannot change his behaviour with any lasting effect.

The conscious mind of a dog, by contrast, is usually a much weaker entity, both as a driver of behaviour or a vehicle to bring about any more lasting change in the way the dog thinks or acts. Yet it is the conscious mind of a dog that we still most commonly try to appeal to in many forms of training. We teach dogs to consciously perform certain tasks, in specific contexts or environments, and think this superficial type of learning will be enough to see them through any number of mental crises later in life, in any number of different contexts, including those where their sub-conscious minds might attempt to exert far greater control over their thinking or reacting.

Understanding sub-conscious 'flooding'

In Book Two of this series, I emphasised how critical it is not just to teach your dog certain exercises, or commands, in specific contexts, such as a training class. You must ensure these commands/exercises are also repeated and reinforced often, and continually, in all manner of different contexts, so that they eventually became programmed not just into his conscious mind, but his sub-conscious mind as well.

For only when your dog's training responses become so much more 'automatic' in any context, or in the face of many different surrounding distractions, do they hold the best hope of seeing him through any later mental crisis. So, even when he is frightened, or feeling threatened, or frustrated, or has an urge to chase something, he will still be able to respond to your commands on a more instinctive level, because the training has become so mentally ingrained.

Readers may also recall that I compared this kind of deeper training and conditioning to how military recruits are prepared for battle. No one just dumps them into a theatre of war until they have first been trained to follow any kind of order without question, and regardless of any competing inner instincts. Otherwise their sub-conscious minds might just compel them to panic and run.

Conversely, if you find yourself in a situation where you are trying to ask your dog to listen to you or respond to a command and he completely ignores you, and continues to react with great agitation, fear, or aggression, this is often down to what I call sub-conscious 'flooding'. In other words, any more conscious thinking ability in your dog has been swept aside by his sub-conscious mind, compelling him to perform these other more instinctive reactions instead.

Another common example of sub-conscious flooding is when a dog goes to a training class and simply will not concentrate on anything that is being said to him by his owner. He may whine or bark instead, or become fearful or highly agitated or even aggressive towards other dogs. This is because his sub-conscious mind has picked up so many stress or threat cues from his immediate environment, on both a sensory and social level, it then compels him to react in a way that wipes out any more conscious thinking or levels of attention.

Regaining better mental control

Really what is happening here, mentally, is that the cart is being put before the horse. The dog first needs to be taught basic commands in the least possible distracting environment, devoid of any of the more sensory or social stress cues that might otherwise limit his greater conscious attention and thus learning. Then this learning has to be constantly repeated, reinforced and ingrained in a steadily building number of different contexts, with a steadily building number of external distractions. Then he is finally able to respond to what he has learned, regardless of the environment he is in or level of surrounding distraction.

Better, deeper or more insightful training is thus often the best – if not the only – tool we really have to hold greater control over our dogs' minds, attention and behaviour when they might otherwise

THE INVISIBLE MOTIVATOR

As the difference between *conscious*, and *sub-conscious*, thinking and actions in animals – including ourselves – might not always be that obvious, it can help to better explain what this difference really is.

The *conscious* mind in animals governs things like everyday environmental awareness, new learning, reasoning and decision-making. And because, as humans, we use conscious thinking a lot during everyday life, we have a tendency to imagine that it represents the bigger, or more influential part of our minds, or indeed any mind.

But in fact, it is the other way round. In all animals – including ourselves – the *sub-conscious* mind is far bigger than the conscious mind. It is also, as earlier outlined, the deeper and more invisible motivator behind so many of our actions and reactions, particularly those linked to memory, impulse and emotion.

Time and again the sub-conscious mind will invade our more conscious thought processes, and drive us to do things, or feel things, without us always understanding why. It can lie at the heart of our most successful survival instincts, but it can also be the driver, too, of many potentially more harmful impulses, such as excess fear or aggression, or more serious forms of addiction. For few sub-conscious minds will ever operate in exactly the same way.

The way I see the difference between the conscious and subconscious mind in animals is like this: the driver and the train. The *conscious* mind is the train driver. The *sub-conscious* mind is the train. Sometimes the driver is able to keep control over the actions of the train. Sometimes the train overrides the driver, and decides to keep going where it wants to go instead.

The latter explains so many occasions in life where the more logical and conscious brain tells us not to do or feel something, but we still feel or do it because we cannot 'stop ourselves'. That feeling of not being able to stop yourself, is when the sub-conscious mind is in control. (*Also see The Battle between your dog's 'two minds' – What's in the sub-conscious mind and how it works, see page 71*).

Excessive vocalisation, or more persistent cycles of barking and whining, is often linked to other mental issues in Collies, like higher neurosis and poorer impulse control. Once begun, and without better training, this habit can also become an increasingly more compulsive reaction for the dog concerned, each or any time he experiences higher mental arousal.

feel compelled to act very differently.

When it comes to training dogs to behave differently, what can also be at stake is the more individual nature of any dog's mind. For we cannot imagine that all Collies have an equal ability to suppress more sub-conscious impulses, or will not have a greater struggle to keep them at bay. Often there are genetic reasons for this, which have to be taken into account, not just to better excuse the dog concerned for his behaviour, but to also make owners feel less of a failure if this behaviour proves far more resistant to their attempts to change it. Genetic tendencies towards poorer impulse control – as highlighted in the next two chapters – can also underpin some of the more serious issues Collies may have with their fear or aggression responses.

More instinctive minds

Once we understand more about instinctive thinking and reacting in dogs, we can also see how wrong it is to imagine that when they engage in more fearful, aggressive or compulsive behaviours, this is always consciously controlled by them. And for the same reason, these behaviours can also seem more 'unreachable' in your dog when you try to do something to stop them.

Very often, for instance, I will see owners trying to soothe dogs who are intensely frightened. But it still makes no difference to their dogs' frightened behaviour. Or I will see owners punish their dogs very harshly for showing aggression or not coming back when called. But it still doesn't stop their dogs from being aggressive again, or not coming back when called again. These were always behaviours performed more instinctively by the dog, and thus behaviours he was less able to consciously control, without far better and more consistent training.

The reason many Border Collies can struggle to exert greater conscious control over their physical responses is because the breed was originally selected, genetically, for traits of higher reactivity and compulsion. These may often work as assets in a working dog, but bring downsides in a social companion, as this series has already amply highlighted.

THE BATTLE BETWEEN YOUR DOG'S 'TWO MINDS'

What's in the sub-conscious mind and how it works

The way to better understand your dog's sub-conscious mind is to see it as an animal's oldest and most primitive survival machine. It triggers all the more instinctive and defensive reactions and impulses (including fear) you need to stay safe and alive, even without consciously thinking about them first.

It also holds a massive database of all the information you need to survive. Like what is safe, or less safe, or more or less rewarding and what it is necessary to be afraid of, or to mount a fear response to. Some of this information (i.e. Pre-birth knowledge, *as outlined in Book 2*) gets handed down directly in DNA from one generation to the next, without having to be 're-learned'.

Other bits of 'survival' information are learned throughout a dog's lifetime, and stored in his sub-conscious mind through the process of memory and mental association. This means a dog will experience something, register a more positive or negative association with it, and then store that lesson in his mind. This lesson will then form the basis for how he will react – i.e. more positively or negatively – whenever he encounters the same experience again.

In every dog, a battle can go on continually between more consciously managed behaviour – including things he knows you want him to do – and more instinctive reactions and compulsions driven by his sub-conscious mind.

Some dogs are naturally better at mastering greater conscious control over inner impulses and compulsions, and others can be taught or conditioned to get better at it (*as outlined in Book Two of this series, and also in the next chapter*). But either way, it is only through appreciating these continual conscious/sub-conscious mind battles in dogs – some of which are won, and others lost – that we start to gain a far more insightful understanding of why any dog won't, or can't, behave as we would like him to.

Tail chasing, spinning and 'shadow chasing' can be common forms of obsessive-compulsive behaviour in the Border Collie.

Obsessive compulsion – or obsessive control?

A more instinctive behaviour which commonly defines the Border Collie, as well as his whole working pattern, is the obsessive repetition of specific actions, such as eyeing, stalking, chasing or herding. Like all behaviour of this kind, it also begins with some initial motivation. Clearly it has its origins in more standard canine hunting behaviour, which then becomes more unnecessarily excessive, or stuck in some less explicable mental loop.

One explanation for why this compulsive behaviour happens in Collies is that it has evolved into a more widespread breed neurosis, linked to a more autistic mind. But to go even deeper, the neurosis, in turn, is also likely to have its roots in *control* – and more precisely the dog's instinctive terror of *losing* control – and thus his need to keep exerting control in other ways.

People who suffer from OCD disorders will frequently tell you that the reason they keep doing the same things again and again, is out of some deeper or more instinctive fear of what might happen to them if they don't, i.e. they might lose control of their own safety in some way, or something bad might happen to them. Even if this fear, to others, may seem pretty irrational, it is very real to them.

Moreover, within the OCD sufferer's mind, the world can often appear so overwhelming as a place of potential threat that only by concentrating on smaller, more immediate patterns of repetitive behaviour can they displace some of the anxiety this causes them and also feel a greater sense of control again.

Once again this is just another example of how the sub-conscious mind powers behaviours in animals, much like ourselves, which appear to defy more conscious logic or control.

Previously in this series I have highlighted how this deeper kind of neurosis and compulsion in Collies, which triggers more repetitive behaviours (including the eyeing, stalking and chasing patterns), is often hardwired into their genetic psychology, as a legacy of their working pasts. As such, you cannot expect to get rid of it. You can only channel it, far more positively, into actions or pursuits over which you can exert far more control as an owner. A subject covered in depth in Book Two of this series.

The level of obsessive behaviour of this kind, found in Collies, can also vary considerably in individual dogs, with dogs from purer working backgrounds or breeding likely to exhibit it more strongly.

A new and different insight

Hopefully this chapter has added further layers of insight into the nature of Border Collies, as a breed.

This is not just in terms of why they are what they are, or do what they do, but how often they may be at the mercy of mental impulses or compulsions that they have a lower ability to consciously control. Much of this may be genetic, but it is also down to how well these dogs are trained and managed from puppyhood so that they are better able to handle situations that might otherwise inspire greater fear, aggression or neurosis. They may then also be able to exert better control over the workings of their own minds.

Having looked at aspects of Collie thinking, and behaviour, that can be far more instinctive or subconscious in origin, in the next couple of chapters we are going to explore the extent to which this might also apply more common fear and aggression problems found in the breed.

'Working' compulsion, or a persistent desire to eye, chase and grab moving objects, comes from the more instinctive part of the Collie mind. It is also an impulse that can switch just as readily from one moving target — such as livestock — to another, such as toys, or even leaves, dust or water.
PHOTO: CAROL PRICE

CHAPTER 8:

FEAR AND ITS FALLOUT

Understanding and managing more fearful Collie behaviour

Every Collie's fear experience will be different in terms of what inspires this sensation, and how they choose to react to it.
PHOTO: CAROL PRICE

Over the years I have read thousands upon thousands of words on the subject of fear and aggression in dogs, and what to do about it, as if it is all pretty similarly inspired behaviour. But what experience has taught me is that, however similar the outward symptoms, no fear or aggression experience, or problem, will ever be exactly the same in any dog.

For each case involves a unique combination of genetic predisposition and learning. It begins where all behaviour begins in all dogs: with the more individual shape and nature of their minds. Why does one particular mind think the way it thinks, and why does it make a dog do what he does?

If you are experiencing some kind of fear or aggression issue with your Collie (*aggression will be covered more fully in the next chapter*), it can be easy to view it as one big stressful concern that eludes any more satisfactory explanation, let alone solution. One of the most stressful aspects of living with dogs who exhibit more acutely fearful or aggressive behaviour – and aggression in particular – is not ever really understanding why a dog is doing what he doing, or feeling able to predict when it might happen again.

So what I am aiming to do, in this chapter, and the next, is to break down the whole mental mechanics of fearful and aggressive behaviours in Collies – and how the two are commonly interlinked – in a way that makes them far more understandable. Thereafter we will be considering the extent to which such behaviours may be better managed in your own dog, or even totally resolved.

This chapter will concentrate primarily on fear as a response in dogs – and Collies in particular – and the next will explore how and why fear of some kind in Collies can so often translate into aggression.

Survival responses

The first thing to understand about fear and aggression in dogs is that they are both perfectly normal survival responses – as they are in most animals, including ourselves – linked to basic defence, protection, and the evasion of threat. So imagining, as some people do, that dogs should go through life totally devoid of these most primal of responses, no matter what the circumstances, is a

little unrealistic to say the least.

The second thing to understand is that there is very little of higher priority to any animal's mind than the act of surviving. That is why responses like fear and aggression are not only deemed so important to the brain, but why it puts the more powerful sub-conscious mind in charge of them. For that way these responses can be activated far more rapidly, and instinctively, even without the conscious mind being greatly involved.

Once we appreciate the extent to which responses like fear and aggression are hardwired into dogs' more instinctive thinking and reacting (as outlined in the last chapter) and, as such, often occur without the dog being able to consciously control them, we also start to better understand the true challenge that can rest in 'curing' dogs of these behaviours – especially longer term. Also see, *What is your dog afraid of and why? - The anatomy of fear.*

A Collie's typical reaction, when faced with scarier sounds like thunder or fireworks is to run to a smaller and more enclosed space to hide in. He may also shake, salivate or pant heavily.
PHOTO: CAROL PRICE

The primal dog mind

More fearful (like aggressive) reactions in dogs may understandably unnerve or concern owners. But really what they are witnessing is the primal brain of the dog taking over, and driving its own instinctive agenda, when it comes to how the dog should react or behave when possessed of a fearful impulse, i.e. shake, freeze, panic, run, hide or attack. We are back to the sub-conscious/conscious mind analogy

WHY IS YOUR COLLIE MORE FEARFUL THAN OTHERS?

People will always yearn for quick fixes to problems like fear and aggression in Collies, when there simply aren't any, because typically they go right to the heart of how a dog is made. Commonly, too, people will wonder why *their* Collie is particularly fearful in his behaviour, especially if they have known, or owned, other Collies who never behaved this way.

As I hope this series has more clearly established, all Collies are different, and possess their own individual package of traits (as outlined in Chapter 2, *The Collie Spectrum*), dating back to the earliest dogs who originally founded the breed. Some of these traits (as covered in Chapter 4, *Knowing your Dog's Mind*), will predispose a dog to have bigger problems with his behaviour in later life, unless he is more expertly reared and trained when younger (as covered in Book Two), or better understood and managed when older.

By focusing, earlier in your dog's life, on the traits likely to give him bigger problems, later on, you stand the best chance of minimising their impact, or even preventing them altogether.

Fear in all animals is ultimately a primal survival response — and some Collies may begin showing it far earlier than others, or experience it more intensely.
PHOTO: CAROL PRICE

I made in the last chapter where, mentally, the train overrides the control of the driver.

That is why dogs, when possessed by these instinctive or sub-conscious impulses, may also seem so unresponsive to any commands you give them to behave differently, as this requires more conscious thought processing.

As covered elsewhere in this series, so many of our relationships with modern dogs are built on the illusion that they have somehow lost all the inner survival impulses and programming that originally defined them as animals, when, in fact, they still exist. It is just that in some dogs some impulses remain stronger than in others, or become attached to more specific things.

Ultimately all that tends to make the difference between a dog's instinctive 'survival thinking' becoming a bigger problem, or not, is how readily and intensely it will trigger the reaction of fear or aggression, and in what contexts.

We may also too readily take for granted a dog's

ability to judge for himself what it is appropriate for him to be frightened of, or aggressive towards. This is instead of seeing it as something that can only result from more extensive social conditioning and training from puppyhood (as covered in Book Two).

Motivation, impulse, physical reaction

People may often see more fearful – or aggressive – behaviour in their Collie as something that happens 'from nowhere' or has a less logical or predictable pattern. But, in fact, there are always three distinct mental stages to fearful or aggressive behaviour in Collies, as in all dogs: namely *motivation*, *impulse* and *physical reaction*. Moreover, these mental stages tend to work in a knock on effect, with one stage rapidly leading to the next, as part of a more instinctive kind of 'survival thinking' previously outlined.

An important thing to understand is that the earlier you can break this mental chain reaction – i.e. at *motivation* stage – the less likely it is that fearful

WHAT IS YOUR DOG AFRAID OF AND WHY?

The anatomy of fear

As anyone knows, fear can be a very personal experience, be this for people, or dogs. You, for example, may not be afraid of what another person is afraid of, and vice versa. Similarly, why one dog may be afraid of a particular thing, and another not, also tends to have more personal reasons.

At the heart of any fear experience in dogs, as in people, lie two basic factors. The first is their personal 'fear data bank'; or what their deeper, sub-conscious minds have chosen to store and/or memorise as more threatening things or experiences. This deeper mental data bank can contain more primal fears, inherited at birth, and also those that have been learned or acquired post birth. For every day your dog is alive, he is being exposed to new environmental 'pictures' around him – both sensory and social – that his mind may choose to store as good, neutral or bad, (i.e. potentially threatening).

How all this environmental information is mentally stored, or categorised, can be a very individual process in dogs. One dog, for instance, might see a child's pushchair or a man wearing a bike helmet and immediately store these pictures as potentially threatening, whereas another will view them as quite neutral, and thus nothing to unduly worry him. One dog may view all visitors to the home as a primarily good, or positive, picture or experience, while another may view the same picture far more negatively. (*Though the latter can often be avoided via the kind of earlier social training outlined in Book Two*).

The second critical – and, again, more individual factor – is how a dog chooses to react whenever a more negative picture he has stored, mentally, is encountered. Will he show initial apprehension, then fairly quickly recover? Or will he shiver, freeze, run, hide or growl, bark or attack? (as outlined under *The primal dog mind*). Both the way a dog chooses to store, and react to, different mental pictures may have some genetic root.

Either way, whatever the dog did the last time he confronted a more negative – or potentially threatening – mental picture, he will attempt to repeat whenever he next encounters it. Because his brain compels him to. This is how dogs get stuck in more persistent cycles of fearful or aggressive behaviour, which often keep rising in frequency or intensity. Also see *Fear contagion*.

Taut body language, lip licking, a tail tucked between the legs and a widened stare can all be signs of rising anxiety in Border Collies.
PHOTO: CAROL PRICE

FEAR CONTAGION, AND FEAR ASSOCIATIONS AND CYCLES

Persistent patterns of fear in Collies begin once the dog has made a negative (i.e. frightening) association with a particular sound/experience and then commits this to memory.

Later he may then behave fearfully not just when exposed to the same fear stimulus again, but also anything that even reminds him of it, or anything that happened just prior to his original fright occurring (a phenomenon known as fear contagion). Commonly the dog may then try to run from his fear source or take refuge in some smaller 'safe space.'

PHOTO BEN WILKES

In the photo (above) the dog is taking emergency refuge in the bathroom shower cubicle in his home because his owners have just opened the top oven grill door in the kitchen. He is afraid of this experience, in turn, because once his owners burnt something under the grill and set off the smoke alarm – creating the noise that was the cause of his initial fright. A classic example of fear contagion.

Fear cycles like these can only be broken once the dog has been taught to have a more positive association with the original source of his fear, i.e. in this case, the oven grill door opening. This can often be successfully achieved with methods like clicker training.

or aggressive impulses and physical reactions will follow. It is the impulse that results from the deeper motivation and, without the impulse from the deeper motivation, the physical reaction doesn't get fired.

As outlined later in this chapter (and also the next, on *Aggression*), sometimes the original motivation for a dog to behave in a more fearful or defensive way will not be so obvious, and thus you have to explore a bit harder to find it.

Fear contagion

As a breed, Collies can often be vulnerable to fear contagion. This is a process whereby one initial fear experience about something particular then progressively spreads to many other contexts which remind the dog, in some shape or form, of the original fear. And each time this happens, the dog then mounts the same level of fear response as he did to the original fear.

A typical example is a dog's fear beginning with a particular sound, or unnerving new experience. He may then widen that fear to any similar sound, or experience, that reminds him in any way of the original frightening incident. Alternatively, if he associates a certain frightening sound or experience with a particular place, he may try to avoid that whole environment later.

Sometimes a dog's fear contagion can be so severe, and encompass so many different contexts, that eventually he will not want to leave the home environment at all. Additionally, dogs may develop a fear about one particular person, or visitor, to the home, and then this spreads to all new visitors he encounters.

It is very important to understand how this process can happen, and spread far beyond the context of an initial fright. To overcome this problem you have to work back in very small steps (as outlined in a moment) beginning with the original fear source for your dog, and changing the sense of threat his mind has attached to it.

Prevention is even better; where you never let one smaller initial fear get bigger for your dog by tackling it the instant it first occurs – with professional help if necessary. Also be aware that you will never have a better chance to turn around a dog's fear about something than when that fear is manifested for the very first time, i.e. well before it has had a chance to spread further, or become increasingly ingrained in his sub-conscious mind.

Tracking back a fear

Due to the vulnerability of Collies to fear contagion – or one initial fear quickly spreading out to encompass many other contexts – owners may not be able to pinpoint the original source of their dog's fear. This, in turn, may make it harder for them to better address or resolve it.

To explain this more fully, I have selected two cases histories: Kirsty, a dog who was frightened of leaving her home (*page 80*), and Ben, a dog who – for no apparent reason– became increasingly fearful (*page 81*). Both stories show that tracking back a fear to its earliest origin and, thus, to its initial motivation, can really help.

A WHOLE NEW APPROACH TO TREATING FEAR

Increasingly – as outlined in the main text – we are understanding how much fear, as well as our responses to it, emanate primarily from the sub-conscious mind. Which is why, to date, treatment for people experiencing more severe fears or phobias has revolved around desensitisation and familiarisation techniques (*of a kind also outlined for dogs with fear issues in the main text*). In other words, an individual is constantly exposed to what they fear, in a more slowly escalating way, to the point where their sub-conscious mind no longer views it as threatening.

Such techniques, if skilfully managed, can often work well for dogs. But the most common stumbling block is usually timing; i.e. recognising early enough when a fear memory is beginning to be triggered in a dog's mind, and then trying to override it with a more positive experience or outcome. For, as outlined in the main text, once a fear memory and impulse takes hold in a dog's mind, he will feel compelled to complete the behaviour that goes with it, and not always possess the conscious ability to behave any differently.

However, neuroscientists from Cambridge University in the UK, plus Japan and the US, have recently developed a whole new approach to this similar problem in humans, with a technique that can help erase fear memories from the sub-conscious mind, even without an individual being consciously aware of this process, or having to be consistently exposed to what they fear.

To do this, they first created a fear memory in selected volunteers by linking pictures they looked at with a mild electric shock. On scans, they then learned to recognise the more exact brain activity in people that was linked to this specific fear memory.

Thereafter, they also discovered that they could see recurrences of this 'fear memory' brain activity even when the volunteers were resting, and thus were not consciously aware of it. And each time they saw this activity, they gave the volunteers some money. The volunteers were never told why they got the money, but later on their fear responses and reactions had dramatically reduced when re-exposed to the pictures that had originally triggered their fear memories.

Obviously such a 'fear curing' technique is still pretty new, and will initially be limited to helping people. However, it does also give us a fascinating new insight into how fear might also be better treated in dogs some time in the future, with far greater effectiveness. Only perhaps with the use of food rewards, rather than money!

KIRSTY: A CASE HISTORY

A little while ago I was called to see a rescue Collie called Kirsty who would not leave the home. She remained rooted to the upstairs landing. Whenever anyone attempted to put a lead on her and take out she simply would not budge, no matter how hard her owners tried to persuade her or tempt her with treats and encouragement. They assumed that Kirsty had just become too frightened to leave the home environment, full stop. Not a lot was known about Kirsty's past history, except that she had formerly been picked up as a stray. She was a noticeably timid dog, but in no way aggressive.

Kirsty's sub-conscious mind had completely 'frozen' her, through fear, to the top of the landing, in a way that made her less able to move for herself. Therefore, I did not speak to her or try to persuade her to move. This can often make the sub-conscious mind of a dog just dig in harder. Instead I simply clipped a lead on her harness and walked her so quickly and confidently down the stairs, with me, with sufficient forward energy, that she had little time to better resist it.

The area around the front door, and the driveway ahead, where her owners' car was parked, was where she showed the greatest reluctance to keep moving. However, once we got beyond that point her movement became freer and freer, to the point where she was soon walking ahead in a calmer and more confident manner. This was at odds with what usually happened in dogs with greater and more widespread social anxieties, who tend to get more panic-struck and reluctant to move

the further they go away from home.

Remembering that Kirsty had been a stray, as well as the fiercer resistance to move she had shown around the front door and driveway area, the thought suddenly struck me that it was the owners' *car in the drive* that was causing her most fear and also greatest reluctance to go out of the front door. She did not want to go past it or near it. Sad to say, many strays are either placed in cars to be dumped, or dumped out of cars into terrifying uncertainty and this can be both a memory and a mental association they do not easily forget.

So I returned home with Kirsty, and asked the owners to move their car out of the drive temporarily, and park it somewhere else. This done, she was immediately far more willing to go out of the front door again and off on her walk.

Following this revelation, we then worked specifically on getting Kirsty more used to the car, and associating it with far more positive experiences. Beginning with just making her walk up nearer and nearer to it and getting a very tasty treat. Then walking away again. Then making her get into the car one side, and immediately out the other for a treat. Then walking away again. Slowly but surely we built up her tolerance of the car until she was happy to get in it and sit in it for longer and longer periods, then get out again when she wanted to.

Today she has no problems whatsoever with the car in the drive, or going out on her walks, which she greatly enjoys.

BEN: A CASE HISTORY

This is the story of Ben, another young Border Collie who suddenly developed greater fear issues.

Ben used to love going for walks on the beach until suddenly, one day, his owners noticed he would not walk past a particular stretch of beach. Every time they tried to call him past it, he would not budge, and instead tried to run back the way they had come, so they were forced to follow him and re-route their walk.

The next day they tried putting him on the lead to walk past this particular stretch of beach. But as soon as they took the lead off he would simply bolt off again with his tail between his legs. Walks on the beach with Ben were becoming not much fun anymore.

Worse was to come later, when Ben then decided he did not want to go *anywhere* near the beach. He had also developed a fear of going out in his owners' garden, and particularly past the outside patio.

I asked Ben's owners if they could think of anything that had triggered his initial fear at the beach. After much deliberating, all they could think of was that one day they were at a cafe and a woman had suddenly scraped back her plastic chair on the concrete, making a loud noise which somewhat startled him. I asked them if the cafe was situated on the stretch of beach where Ben had shown his earlier reluctance to go. Yes. I also asked them if, on their garden patio, they had similar plastic chairs to the ones at the beach cafe. Yes.

A lightbulb moment. The whole fear problem had begun with a scraping plastic chair, and then rippled progressively outward to any environment containing a similar kind of plastic chair.

Again, we had to work our way back to the beginning. The beach cafe was closed for winter, so we had to take our own plastic chair down there, together with a dog whose mood continually wavered from high anxiety to all out bafflement.

We began by seeing how far away we could place the chair, and scrape it back, without Ben reacting more fearfully. It was a long, long way away at first, but then the more and more we did it, the closer we could get to him, and scrape it, without him reacting fearfully. And each time he did not react fearfully we rewarded him with a tasty treat. We also did the same with the patio chairs at home. On and on it went for several days, with his owners scraping plastic chairs back and forward, again and again, until Ben was not so much anxious about them as absolutely sick of the sound of them.

Moreover, it finally got to the point where when anyone put a hand on a plastic chair, he instantly sat there waiting for a treat, completely bypassing the fearful reaction stage altogether. Which is exactly what we wanted. For Ben's sub-conscious mind had now completely reworked its previous negative perception of plastic chairs and decided they were no longer threatening.

Not long after that Ben was back enjoying his walks on the beach again, and had no problems about going back in the garden, or past the patio.

Sensory fears

As already highlighted in this series, the Border Collie can be prone to a number of both social and sensory fears, due to the nature of his particular brain design and psychology. In the latter case, it can be common for Collies to develop fears or phobias about certain noises.

As a rule, I tend to place noise fears in Collies into two different categories, which are driven by two different motivations. There are those related to sounds which cause the dog actual sensory and physical pain. Thus the *pain* the dog has experienced from these sounds in the past forms the *motivation* for his more fearful *impulses* and *physical* reactions to them later.

Then there are sounds which the dog mentally connects to more negative experiences or events. In other words, it is not the sound, in itself, that causes the *motivation* for the dog's later fear *impulses* and *physical reactions*, but *the more negative experience he has come to connect the sound with in his mind*.

'Brain pain' noises

When it comes to sensory discomfort caused by sound, as outlined earlier in this series, we don't always realise how much actual physical pain many louder environmental noises cause dogs, because their hearing, and levels of sensory awareness, are far more acute than our own. And Collies can have higher sensory acuity than most.

We have a tendency, in general, to judge sound more in terms of how we are personally perceiving it, rather than through the more amplified sensory systems of other animals. It is only just being realised, for example, how agonising the sound of things like humans screams or clapping can be to performing dolphins at marine zoos, because their echo-locating auditory systems are geared to registering the most minimal sound frequencies underwater, and thus are exceptionally acute.

In the list of noises that could cause your Collie physical 'brain pain' could be household items like power drills, vacuum cleaners, lawnmowers, televisions and even food mixers. Externally they will include things like thunder, fireworks, trains and traffic – particularly bigger vehicles with air brakes, like trucks, or motorbikes.

If a noise causes you some degree of sensory and physical pain, it makes pretty good sense for your mind to fear its reoccurrence, and instruct you to avoid it in the future. Or, if you cannot do that, find a place to better escape or hide from it, or react more defensively (like barking) to try to make it go away. Which is what a lot of dogs tend to do.

However, if they run or hide or bark – but the painful noise keeps continuing – their fear response systems may then go into overdrive. Causing classic symptoms like uncontrollable shaking, shivering, hyper-ventilating, panting or hyper-salivation. It can be very distressing to witness a dog in this state.

Some Collies may also try to deflect the mental/sensory discomfort caused by louder or more alarming noises into aggression towards others, such as in classic lunge-nip behaviour.

Dealing with 'brain pain' noises

The trouble with louder 'brain pain' noises of any kind is that as long as they are continuing to cause the dog pain, it is hard to convince, or better persuade, his sub-conscious mind that he shouldn't react to them in an adverse way.

So the first thing you have to ask yourself, when it comes to louder noises in the home, is how essential it is that your dog is exposed to them. When instead he could be allowed to go – or be put – somewhere a lot quieter where he is not exposed to them. Thus lowering the motivation for him to react in a more fearful or threatened way.

I say this, because people continually tell me things like: "Our dog never likes staying with us in the sitting room – how can we make him stay with us?" The most common reason why Collies don't like the sitting room is the television. It is frequently too loud for them, or generally causes them some level of sensory distress, including excess light and movement. It may also be why they often bark at it.

Your dog does not have to be exposed to the television. So if he doesn't want to be exposed to the television, or the vacuum cleaner, or the lawnmower or power drill, and these devices keep prompting more reactive or agitated behaviour in him, why not just let him go or be somewhere else a lot quieter instead?

As a rule, if your dog is trying to evade, or is reacting more excessively to, any noise made by anything in your home, it is pretty much always because he is finding it distressing in some way. So let him have the option of not being exposed to it if you can. Also remember to create his own special refuge zone (*as mentioned earlier in this series*), where he can go for greater peace, and see the Chapter 10, *Sensory Detox*, for more advice on keeping dogs calmer in the home.

Sometimes when a dog shows some early aversion to a household noise, what can happen instead is that an owner puts increasing pressure on him to face it again and again, in order to get him 'more used to it', before his sub-conscious mind has adapted sufficiently to make this step (see, *Desensitisation and familiarity*). This often leads to a dog getting even more anxious about the noise.

WHEN DOES A FEAR BECOME A PHOBIA?

Survival responses that get out of control

The way to look at any fear response system in an animal –including ourselves – is much like the immune system. When it is working efficiently it mounts a response to threat that is adequate for survival, then quickly returns to more balanced functioning again.

When it is working less efficiently, or more over-actively, it can cause far greater havoc within the mind and body of any individual. Just as animals with more over-active immune systems can suffer a range of serious health problems, those with more over-active fear or anxiety response systems can suffer a far higher level of stress. This can be of a kind that affects them both mentally and physically, and also severely disrupt the quality of their everyday lives.

We do not always know why some animals are able to keep their fear or anxiety responses under better control, whereas others are not. Or why in some animals an initial fear about something then spirals rapidly into an all-consuming terror which seems totally out of proportion, threat-wise, to the original stimulus that triggered it. But there may well be some genetic element involved. And certainly in some Collies it may be linked to their generally more reactive psychologies, more acute sensory perception and poorer impulse control.

When a fear response spirals totally out of control in this way, however, it becomes a phobia.

Desensitisation and familiarity

As outlined in *A whole new approach to treating fear (page 79)* some exciting new possibilities may lie ahead with regard to the treatment of excess, or more inappropriate, fear in people and maybe also, one day, animals. But for now, in dogs, we remain stuck with more traditional methods of persuading their sub-conscious minds to feel differently about things they have previously found frightening.

And this includes noises they are less able to avoid, like thunder or fireworks. The reason why these can hold a particular terror for dogs is not just because of how loud – and thus painful – they can be for them, on a sensory level, but also because they are far more unpredictable in occurrence. This lack of predictability, or more on-going occurrence, means the dog's brain is less able to get used to the sound or experience of them, or find them increasingly familiar, and thus less threatening.

So a way to make your dog feel better about them, and louder noises in general, is through a more gradual process of desensitisation and familiarity, using one of the commercial 'scarier sounds' DVDs now around. You start by playing these sounds – which usually include thunder and fireworks – at a very low volume, and on a far more regular basis, in many different contexts. Then very gradually up the volume, only as and when your dog is able to cope with this without displaying any fear.

If this is not working well, then it could be because you are turning the volume of a noise up too high, and/or too soon, before your dog's mind and sensory systems have had sufficient chance to adapt. Or you are not replicating the sound enough times daily for your dog to adapt in the same way. Or you may not be playing the sound in enough varieties of context, including both outside as well as inside the home.

If your dog, for instance, learns to tolerate a louder banging noise inside the home, he may not have the same level of tolerance to it outside the home, because he has not gone through the same kind of familiarisation procedure with it in this context. Thus, play the sounds everywhere.

Distraction techniques can also work well. And this is where, whenever you recreate a sound your dog has previously been worried about, you also immediately direct his attention on to a toy he particularly likes and allow him to play with it, before he has had the chance to become more fearful. Which can ultimately lead to him making a more positive – or less worrying – mental connection with the same noise later on.

Collies can vary considerably in terms of how well they may respond to these kind of 'brain pain' noise desensitisation techniques. It can also depend on how good a sensory filter they might possess; i.e. an ability to screen louder noises more into the mental background over time, due to the frequency with which they hear them. Much in the way people who live near airports eventually stop noticing the sound of passing planes.

Some Collies may find it a lot harder to do this because their brains are less able to apply this kind of filter system which, in turn, would protect them from the effects of more excessive sensory discomfort or stress. Also see Chapter 10, *Sensory detox*, for more advice on this.

Noises and bad associations

As mentioned earlier, as well as fears dogs may have, or develop, about 'brain pain' sounds, they can also develop a fear of certain noises with which they have made a more negative mental connection. Thus the negative memory connected to a sound is the triggering motivation for their fearful behaviour.

A common example is the sound of rain. Collies may fear it because they have come to mentally connect it to the even scarier prospect of thunder. Or the sound of a telephone ringing. It is usually not the

sound of the telephone ringing, in itself, that causes anxious or agitated behaviour in some Collies, but the more sudden changes in their owners' behaviour that immediately follow this sound. This could be physically rushing to answer the phone, if it is a landline. Or instantly switching off all attention from the dog to speak to someone he cannot see. Thus, your dog connects the sound of the phone with a more disturbing immediate change in your normal behaviour.

Another example of a noise linked to a negative experience is flies. People can imagine that their dog is terrified of the sound of flies when it is really what he connects the sound of flies to; i.e. his owner swatting them with something like a newspaper.

So be aware of the way sounds can trigger a more fearful response in your dog, simply because of the experience he connects them to. And consider what you might do to change this. In the case of the rain, try sound desensitisation techniques already highlighted. In the case of the telephone, always take calls somewhere away from your dog if he reacts adversely, so that he is less able to be affected by any sudden change in your behaviour. Or place him somewhere else when you take the call.

Similarly in the case of flies, put your dog somewhere else out the way if you intend to swat them. It is not exactly rocket science, but it can make a fair deal of difference to your dog's stress levels.

Understanding fear cycles

People often think of fear in dogs as being something that goes up, and then down, as a response or, at least, has a pretty linear process from beginning to end. But dogs can also get stuck in longer lasting cycles of fear, which drive them to keep repeating the same loops of more 'frozen' or reactive behaviour again and again. Such fear cycles can last from minutes to hours and it can help to better understand them.

Here is a typical example of a fear cycle in action. Recently I came across a woman sitting on a rock, with her dog about four feet away from her. She said she had been there *two hours* trying to catch her dog, but every time she moved towards him to grab him he ran away again. I asked her to walk off some distance away from her dog, and when she did so

Tolerating the new: Fear responses in individual Collies may have some genetic basis, but still the more novel experiences you expose your dog to, at an early age, and in a positive way, the more he will be able to cope with later in life, without experiencing anxiety.
PHOTO: CAROL PRICE

he immediately followed, through still keeping the critical four feet gap between them, and dodging any attempt she or anyone else made to get closer or quickly grab him.

It was clear the owner was very, very angry and frustrated. Because she thought the dog's behaviour was being motivated by sheer bloody-mindedness or defiance, when to me it was more obviously –from the dog's body language – being motivated by fear. I asked the owner if she had ever been very angry and hostile to the dog in the past, when she had finally grabbed him after he had not come back quickly. I could see immediately from her face not only that she had, but that her reaction had been something more excessive in the way of violence. And her dog knew that, too.

Thus his sub-conscious mind had retained a picture of his owner when she was in a certain mood or approaching him closely, in a certain way, to grab him, and connected it to a very frightening past experience. Meaning every time he saw this picture again, he was instinctively compelled to physically evade his owner, and the potential threat to come, even if he may have wanted to stay with her on a more conscious level. So on and on this conscious/sub-conscious mental stalemate went, for hours, with the dog continually driven to evade his owner whenever she got a certain distance away from him. And it would never stop happening until the *motivation* for it happening stopped, i.e. her more hostile body language/behaviour when trying to catch her dog, or after she had caught her dog.

I went up far more slowly and benignly to the dog and, in a pretty short period of time, just gently took his collar, then gave him a treat. It had never occurred to the dog's owner that his more evasive behaviour was motivated by fear, or why. I'd like to think it does now. *Please also be aware that Book Two in this series – and particularly Chapter 7, on Recall – gives detailed advice on how to avoid these kinds of problems with your own dog, through more insightful training.*

Fear cycles about noise – like thunder or fireworks – can also work the same way, in that every time the dog hears the sound of them again, he repeats a new fear response again, so the fearful behaviour appears to occur in one more continuous loop. Moreover, the dog cannot stop this reaction until he is able to more successfully escape the noise, mentally tolerate the noise, or the noise stops. See *Desensitisation and familiarity* (*page 83*) for more advice on dealing with such noises.

The value of persistence

One of the commonest reasons why fear responses in Collies continue – other than just the more stubborn refusal of their sub-conscious minds to surrender them – can be a lack of persistence in addressing the problem.

If a dog has a fear problem you do not share, or fail to adequately understand, it can be all too easy to become impatient or exasperated with him, and try to rush or more heavily pressurise him out of it – faster than his mind is prepared to go. This, in turn, can cause extra anxiety in him, which holds up further progress.

It is important to remember the need to first isolate, most accurately, the true initial source of your dog's fear – as just outlined – and also to tackle it in one small step of progress at a time, rather than at a pace that may be more preferable to you. It is always better to make two or three small steps of progress in a dog's fear problem, and consolidate these before moving on. If you rush him too far, too soon – beyond what his mind can comfortably cope with – you can often make the problem worse.

A 'small step' could just simply be getting your dog a bit nearer to something 'scary' than he would go before. Or your dog being able to tolerate a noise at a slightly higher volume – see *Sensory fears* – than he could tolerate before.

Curing dogs of fear problems can be hard work, there is no denying it. But so can living with a dog whose fear behaviours get progressively worse and worse. Some dogs will always take longer to change their attitudes, or responses, to things they previously found frightening. But you still have to let their minds decide for themselves when that point is, however long it takes, in order to bring about any more lasting kind of improvement in their behaviour.

Fear avoidance

Another common obstacle to better resolving fears in dogs, or preventing them from further escalating, is an owner's temptation to keep avoiding things that make their dog afraid. In order to avoid, in turn, the often more challenging behaviour that tends to accompany this; i.e. the dog becoming more agitated, hysterical or aggressive, or trying to run away.

Though a totally understandable temptation, the upshot of such constant avoidance of fear triggering contexts or events is that the owner ends up colluding with their dog's sub-conscious mind, and its more personal perception of threat, rather than encouraging it to think or react any differently. Which means the behaviour not only continues but very often gets steadily worse.

So sometimes it is owners, and not just dogs, who have to find the courage within themselves to face challenging situations like these more head on; to ride the storm of fear with their dog and help him go through it to a better place on the other side. Rather than continue to be stuck in the same mental prison as their dog, never knowing what life might have been like if they had both been able to make more effort to get out of it.

Having explored fear as an emotion, and survival response, in dogs, where it comes from in the mind, how it gets stored there and why dogs may respond to it so differently, we are now going to move on to fear's more evil twin – aggression.

Aggression in Collies may often be a more harmless part of play behaviour (as in this photo) but at other times it can have more complex motivations, and also, potentially, more serious outcomes.

The way to view aggression in dogs is as the end product of a problem that started earlier in the brain. For example, the dog's far readier perception of threat, and/or lower ability to contain emotions such as fear, anxiety or frustration, so that they keep exploding outwards into physical reactions.

Physical reactions to higher emotional or mental pressure won't always be aggression in Collies. Sometimes they may just be more extreme agitation or hyper-excitability, like excessive barking and jumping and spinning around, or more compulsive patterns of obsessive activity. But in dogs whose brains think aggression is the most appropriate reaction to mental pressure, aggression is likely to be more common.

From the outset in this chapter I would like to say that the majority of Border Collies do not have aggression issues. However, that is not much help if you happen to be an owner whose dog does have an aggression issue, and this chapter is more specifically for owners like these, or anyone who would like to understand Collie aggression a bit better.

If you do have a Collie with some kind of aggression issue, it can really help to begin by seeing the problem in the following way. Perceive it as something that frequently begins with your dog's whole mental wiring, rather than something you have wholly created yourself, through your poorer handling or socialisation of your dog when he was younger. Lots of dogs do not get the best start in life, but still do not become aggressive when they are older.

Aggression due to a heightened sense of vulnerability: The smaller a space a Collie is confined in — such as, in this case, a car — the more vulnerable he will feel, and thus more motivated to defend himself, when suddenly approached by others he knows less well. The same sense of heightened vulnerability, prompting more defensive behaviour, may arise in dogs when they are tied up, on the lead, in pain or find themselves more clearly 'trapped' somewhere without a more obvious escape route, such as in the vet surgery.

PHOTO: CAROL PRICE

AGGRESSION – AND A MORE DANGEROUS CANINE MIND MODEL

In the human world there can be many people possessing – much like Collies – specific mental traits that cause them greater problems in life. These include a capacity to resort too readily to aggression when under mental pressure, or to react to a perceived threat that did not really exist.

The consequences are not always pretty for those at the other end of their reactions. People with these kinds of more incendiary mental qualities may also struggle to have healthier social relationships or, at the worse end of the scale, end up in prison as a result of physical assaults on others, or even murders, or any other number of more reckless or violent crimes and behaviours that were launched impulsively in "the heat of the moment".

In other words, they just could not "stop themselves" from doing what they did.

They can also have another trait in common, often termed as 'problems with authority'. But actually it is not authority, per se, they have the greatest mental struggle with, but *control*. Or, more specifically, they have a deeper reluctance to be controlled by others, and a higher need to control others themselves.

When you put all these mental qualities together, you can see how it produces a potentially dangerous mind model in people. But for some reason we seem to imagine that such a mind model is restricted purely to humans, and cannot also manifest itself in other animals or their behaviour, albeit it in a more primitive form.

Yet, time after time, in aggressive dogs – both Collies and others breeds – I have seen basically the same kind of mind model producing much the same kind of behaviour, with much the same pretty dire consequences. This is not just for the individuals affected by the dog's aggression, but for the dog himself. In terms of the poorer quality of his own life and social relationships, and the risk he may face down the line of being euthanased – for prison is no available option for dogs.

Moreover, by failing to better recognise the link between this kind of dangerous mind model in dogs – likely to have a genetic root – and more persistent or serious aggression problems in them, we can never get closer to breeding dogs without it, which would give both them and their owners far less troubled lives.

Deflected aggression: Excess mental arousal in Collies — such as that caused by anxiety, frustration, excitement or sensory overload — can trigger a knock-on defence reaction in them, which then gets directed on to the nearest available target. This may include other dogs, or even people, the dog lives with. Often dogs will get judged harshly for this behaviour when, in reality, it is often an instinct, or reflex, over which they have very little conscious control. Behaviours like these in dogs, however, can be greatly lessened by giving them better all round training in impulse control
PHOTO: CAROL PRICE

Aggression motivators

In Chapter 4, *Knowing your Dog's Mind*, I highlighted some inherent qualities in Collies that could heighten the risk of them becoming aggressive later in life. Namely:

1. *Greater fear or intolerance of the new*
2. *Control neuroses prompting more obsessive defence of personal space and resources*
3. *Lower social awareness or recognition*
4. *Poor impulse control*

And to these qualities I would also add:

5. *A deeper need, in general, to control others*
6. *Higher social anxiety, in general; i.e. the dog views his world, more widely, as a constant source of different threats*
7. *Greater vulnerability to sensory overload*

But on top of all these you will still need that all important extra element which is:

8. *A dog whose most natural response to mental pressure is....aggression*

Thus these are some of the commonest *motivations* for mental pressure in Collies which thereafter – in dogs more inclined to this reaction – trigger the aggressive *impulses* and *physical reactions* that then ensue. These operate in a similar sort of *motivation-impulse-physical reaction* chain sequence as with fear behaviours, in the last chapter.

For fear – if not terror – of new things can cause great mental pressure and anxiety in a dog. So can a mindset convinced that the world is an unremittingly scary or threatening place. And so can anything that threatens a dog's more intense – if not obsessive – need to retain or exert control over his immediate personal space or resources.

A lower understanding of social communication and behaviour adds further pressure, as the dog is less able to distinguish between more benign social signals in other dogs or people and more hostile ones (see *Dogs and the pressures of poorer social awareness, page 97*).

If we add poorer impulse control to mounting mental pressure, it is it easy to see why aggression can so often be the end result in a dog. Additionally some dogs (as outlined in *Aggression – and a more dangerous canine mind model*) are born with more incendiary personalities that can also make aggression more of a problem in them.

So we are beginning to realise that cases of aggression in Collies may not be as random or inexplicable in nature as we previously considered; they may not even be to do with botched rearing or handling on the part of owners. Instead, they may well be more rooted in the kind of genetic mind model a dog inherited at birth, revolving around patterns of deeper anxiety, higher reactivity and a more obsessive desire for control.

If we look further back in the breed's earliest history – covered in Book One of this series – we can also better understand how some Collies came to inherit a more challenging kind of mind model in the first place. Much of the breed's original livestock work demanded far higher levels of mental reactivity in a dog, and a more compelling need to both pursue and maintain control.

Nobody considered around a century ago, however, how the genetic perpetuation of traits like these in Collies might later impact on the quality of their lives and relationships with others, in a far more socially demanding future world.

Aggression prevention

There is only one fool-proof way to ensure you do not have a Collie who displays aggression problems in later life. Get one whose inherent genetic make-up does not feature any of the mental vulnerabilities, neuroses, fears or obsessions I mentioned earlier (under *Aggression motivators*) at a more extreme level, plus the all-important additional instinct to respond to these pressures in a more aggressive way.

If you already have a dog with a more aggression-prone mindset, then another strategy for reduced aggression is to micro-manage his daily life, and environment, to such a precise degree, that all the mental pressure triggers that might otherwise fire his aggression never get pushed. This is less than ideal, and potentially far more stressful, as any owner who has lived through such micro-managing

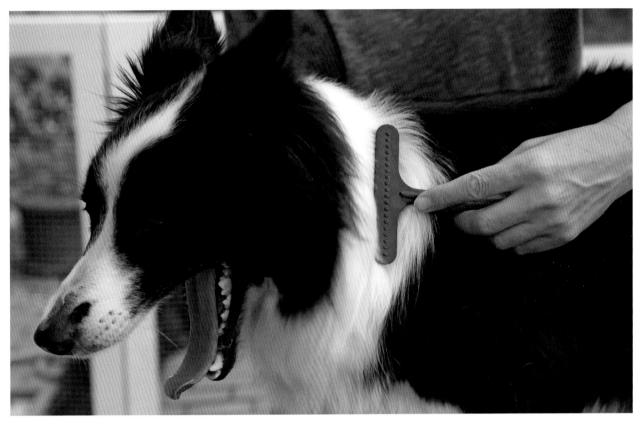

Warning signs: Some Collies may find more intimate and physical human approaches – such as hugging, grabbing or grooming – highly uncomfortable, as they threaten their deeper need to maintain control of their personal space. Yawning, growling or tensing up can be earliest signs that your dog may mount some defensive response when placed under pressure in this way.

of their Collie and his behaviour might attest. And I have known quite a few of them.

Then in-between there are greyer areas of compromise where, given your dog's essential mindset, you do all you can to stretch his social tolerance, and levels of impulse control, to keep any more aggressive reactions checked, through better training and management. It is also important to appreciate that any Collie who has displayed aggression once, especially with minimal provocation, will always be capable of displaying it again.

Also be aware that, as with fear episodes (highlighted in the last chapter) every aggression episode in a Border Collie will be different, involving a personal combination of genetic disposition and learning. Plus something more specific that was happening in a dog's mind, or environment, at a particular time, sufficient to trigger the aggressive impulse or reaction.

Breeding 'for temperament'

As long as I have been around Border Collies I have listened to breeders talking about how vital it is to breed dogs with 'sound' temperaments. And yet every day more and more Collies with less sound temperaments, and their owners, turn up at my door needing help.

Sometimes this is simply down to some breeders not caring enough about the mental quality of the dogs they produce. Or not making it a greater genetic priority, especially in Collies destined to be social companions. At other times they do care, but are just less able to spot the 'warning bell' genetic qualities in dogs (outlined earlier) that so often lead to later problems, or understand their wider significance. They may also not understand how the more persistent inbreeding of dogs so often leads to serious deteriorations in their genetic temperaments, or wider mental health.

However, such factors remain major contributors

to the perpetuation of aggression and temperament problems in all dog breeds today.

Better early assessments of dogs

As outlined in Chapter 2 (*The Collie Spectrum*) and Chapter 4 (*Knowing your Dog's Mind*), earliest possible assessments of your dog's inherent temperament, and mental outlook, can also help immensely in preventing future aggression problems. For as these chapters highlighted, once you are aware of traits likely to inspire aggression in a Collie, before they have become a problem, you can use more appropriate training and management of your dog to further reduce the chance of this happening.

Dogs may initially show their unease in signals like yawning, or cowering, or attempting to more obviously evade being held or caught. It is only when these signals are consistently ignored that they may resort to more defensive physical reactions, such as growling, teeth baring or snapping.

It is always better to recognise this kind of anxiety trait in your dog as early as possible, and then work on teaching him more positive responses towards human contact. Otherwise the problem will escalate, to the point where your dog becomes progressively more aggressive towards you, each time you threaten to invade his space.

Also be aware that, as with fear behaviour, you will never have a better opportunity to reverse or cure aggressive behaviour in Collies than from the moment when it first starts – and employing appropriate professional help is also recommended. This is to prevent the behaviour becoming further rewarded, reinforced and ingrained into the dog's mind, through a deeper on-going learning process which I am now about to outline.

How genetics and learning influence aggression in dogs

As with fear behaviour, aggressive behaviour in Collies, as in most dogs, usually begins with some deeper genetic motivation, i.e. the behaviour is more instinctive in origin. Then over time it will acquire some more learned elements, as the dog better discovers the effects of his aggressive behaviour on others, or how it makes him feel inside.

If the effects continue to be positive in some way for the dog – i.e. solving a problem by making a threat go away, or causing an immediate release of his inner mental tension – then he will file the aggressive behaviour away in his mind as an essentially more rewarding and appropriate response. And, thus, it will be something, thereafter, he will become progressively more motivated to keep repeating.

It is important to understand that this kind of learning often happens sub-consciously in a dog. Owners may be similarly unaware of what their dog has learned and mentally stored from his previous aggression episodes, or why he has found aggression so rewarding, which can also make it harder for them to understand why his aggression keeps persisting.

Having looked at the different origins and motivations of aggression in Collies, let us now look at commoner aggression problems in the breed, as well as how they might best be addressed.

Please note: While I may now be outlining my own approaches to different types of aggression in Border Collies, and some advice which may also help you, any aggression problem in any dog should first always be assessed and addressed by a suitably experienced and qualified canine behaviourist. Similarly, any rehabilitation training for aggressive dogs – including the use of deterrents – should always be supervised by an experienced, qualified behaviourist.

Aggressive dogs can sometimes be dangerously unpredictable. Or their problems may worsen with inexperienced or inappropriate handling. That is why you should never try to tackle an aggression problem in a dog entirely by yourself, without expert professional supervision and help.

Lunge-nip aggression

One of the most common forms of aggression found in Border Collies is the lunge-nip type, typically where the dog will quickly lunge outwards or upwards and maybe even growl, snap or attempt to bite when something moves into his head space, or suddenly approaches.

People often consider this a misdirected 'working' instinct in Collies. It is, in terms of the use such a rapidly fired defence response can be for a dog, when subjected to the threat or challenge of approaching livestock. However, it is also an instinct firmly linked to mental pressure, including those mentioned earlier in this chapter, i.e.:

- *Greater fear or intolerance of the new.*
- *Control neuroses prompting more obsessive defence of personal space and resources.*
- *Lower social awareness or recognition.*
- *A deeper need, in general, to control others.*

In other words, any of all of these mental pressure points, or any stimuli triggering higher emotional states in your dog (i.e. fear, excitement, frustration, anxiety) are more likely to trigger lunge-nip behaviour in him, especially in dogs who also have inherently *poorer impulse control*.

So if, for instance, an approaching dog or person is less familiar to your dog, and this frightens him, or he is less able to read whether they have a benign or hostile body language, he is more likely to lunge-

Lunge-nipping at household objects: More reactive/defensive 'lunge-nip' instincts in Collies can also get unleashed on moving objects such as brooms, mops or vacuum cleaners.
PHOTO: CAROL PRICE

Lunge-nipping at people and traffic: Objects that pass the Collie's eye level at speed — such as cyclists, runners or traffic — often trigger his natural 'pursuit and defence' reflexes, as a sheepdog. He may thus more instinctively chase or lunge out at them, without appropriate training to keep such impulses under better control.
PHOTO: CAROL PRICE

nip at them. The more your dog needs to control his space or resources, the more likely he is to indulge in this behaviour if suddenly approached closely. This is especially likely if he is in possession of resources he most prizes, such as food – *note, Food guarding aggression* is covered on *page 100.*

It could be more strategic bits of household territory, such as the front door area, hallway or top of the stairs, or where his bedding is situated. Or when he is trapped in smaller spaces which he feels more compelled to defend from the approach of others, such as inside the car. Also see, *Dealing with space and territory related aggression, page 102.*

Different forms of sensory stress, or overloading – or the dog being hit by an overwhelming source of noise, movement or crowding – can also trigger lunge-nip behaviour. This is why a Collie may direct it at traffic or household objects, or even at owners, sometimes, if he is suffering sensory distress and there is no more appropriate object to deflect his ensuing aggressive impulse on to.

I tend to see lunge-nip behaviour in Collies as an issue primarily revolving around *impulse control.* In the sense that, regardless of the mental pressure provoking a dog to lunge-nip, the problem could still be better contained if the dog was able to exert greater conscious control over his own physical responses (see, *Teaching better impulse control*). In more persistent cases of inappropriate lunge-nipping, some kind of additional deterrent, like a spray collar, may also be needed, to better deter the dog from this kind of behaviour. Also see, *When and how should deterrents be used to address an aggression problem?, page 95.*

Deterring and retraining the lunge-nipper

As outlined a little later in *When and how should deterrents be used to address an aggression problem?*, not all aggression problems in dogs can be solved with reward-based techniques alone, depending on how strongly the dog is motivated, or driven, to react aggressively. For often the impulse will override all conscious thinking in a dog, including his ability to concentrate on any reward or an

alternative command you may be trying to offer him, in order to better prevent or stop his aggressive behaviour.

In situations like these you will need something extra to try to shock or interrupt the dog's sub-conscious mind out of its intended course of action, i.e. to mount and complete an aggressive physical response. I prefer to use a remote control spray collar, which emits a disconcerting, but by no means harmful, sudden puff of air.

Moreover, timing in this kind of deterrent work is absolutely critical, in that you have to interrupt the aggressive impulse while it is still a *thought* in the dog's mind and *before* it has had a chance to be

---

TEACHING BETTER IMPULSE CONTROL

Repeatedly in this series I have highlighted how vital it is to understand the relevance of levels of impulse control in Border Collies. The less control a dog is able to master over his own behaviour, and particularly his physical responses to inner impulses or emotions, the more of a problem his behaviour is likely to become.

As outlined in the main text, poor impulse control can be a prime motivator of aggression in Collies. But it can also impinge on other wider mental aspects in the dog, like his general levels of focus and concentration, or ability to settle and rest. Dogs with poorer impulse control can also get stuck in more manic, on-going loops of self-stimulatory or obsessive behaviour, from which they seem unable to escape.

There can, undoubtedly, be a genetic aspect to levels of higher or lower impulse control in Collies. And, as highlighted in Chapter 2 (*The Collie Spectrum*), University of Lincoln's School of Life Sciences, in the UK, did a recent study revealing that poorer impulse control was significantly more common in Collies from working lines, as opposed to those from show bred lines.

However, it is definitely a mental aspect

that you can progressively improve in your dog with better training, as covered specifically in Book Two of this series (Chapter 4, *focus, co-operation and impulse control*).

To recap, such training involves you asking your dog to better *focus* and also *wait*, for progressively longer periods, before getting anything more rewarding, such as his food, or in situations where he might otherwise get over-excited, such as just before a walk. Too often I will see Collies consistently allowed to act out their every emotion or impulse, in ever more manic ways, without any brake being installed on this process, in the form of greater mental self-discipline.

The more relentlessly you teach Collies greater impulse control, the better and better they tend to get at it, and the benefits can also then feed into wider aspects of their behaviour, including levels of responsiveness to commands.

Do be aware, however, of additional factors that can compromise a dog's levels of impulse control, and render him far more reactive and defensive in his responses. These include the dog being under exceptional mental stress – be this sensory or psychological – or suffering from some source of physical pain. All of this needs to be addressed before his impulse control levels can return to a healthier setting.

WHEN AND HOW SHOULD DETERRENTS BE USED TO ADDRESS AN AGGRESSION PROBLEM?

In an ideal world we would never have to use deterrents of any kind to resolve less acceptable or desirable behaviours in dogs. We would only use reward-based methods – and that remains the preferred course of action in dogs where it is most likely to work.

In some dogs, however, the impulse to be aggressive, fired by the sub-conscious mind, is so strong that it completely overwhelms their entire thinking and behaviour, leaving them less able to make more conscious choices as to how they should behave. The sub-conscious mind will not allow the option to surrender aggression, in return for a reward, as long as it still believes that aggression is the most necessary course of action in a particular context.

Thus it is only when aggression, as a response and strategy, has proven to be consistently less rewarding or effective for the dog – via the additional involvement of deterrents – that his sub-conscious mind begins to function differently. Aggression as an option, in short, has to consistently fail, again and again, before the dog can start considering other options that might be more rewarding.

Any deterrent, however, must always be used hand in hand with additional on-going retraining of the dog in all of his former 'flashpoint' contexts, so that these become ever less worrying or threatening to him. He must also be consistently rewarded for showing greater tolerance or confidence, instead of aggression. Additionally the more skilfully a deterrent is used, the less often it has to be employed to bring about the most successful results.

Leave it to the professionals: Devices such as a remote control spray collar (pictured), to help deter aggression in dogs, typically fail to solve the problem longer term because owners use them incorrectly in terms of timing, context or over-use. They are thus best only employed by canine professionals.
PHOTO: CAROL PRICE

translated into an actual *physical reaction*. If you use it too early, you may be attaching the deterrent to the wrong, or more harmless, thought or intention in his mind, not only making him confused but potentially giving him new hang-ups about things he never had before.

If you use it as the dog is actually *being* aggressive, or even *after* he has been aggressive, it is too late. The aggressive impulse has already escaped into a physical reaction and thus all the deterrent effect has been lost.

So if you have tried to use a spray collar on your dog in the past to stop his aggressive reactions, only for it not to work, it is likely to be your timing, or

reading of your dog, that is most at fault. Owners can also hideously over-use these devices on their dogs, to the point where they become progressively less effective, through losing their initial shock value in the dog's mind.

Thus, for all these reasons, I recommend that use of spray collars should be confined to a professional and suitably qualified behaviourist or trainer, or under their more direct supervision.

Aborting the lunge–nip impulse

If used correctly, such deterrents can suitably halt a dog in his tracks just before he is about to perform a lunge-nip reaction towards a favoured target (e.g.

traffic, cyclists, passing dogs or people). They also create a temporary mental pause in the dog's head, and return to some improved conscious thinking. At this point you can immediately invite him to perform an alternative behaviour – like *sit* and *watch me* – *instead* of lunge-nipping. When he responds to this you can fulsomely praise him and give him some really tasty treats or a favourite toy, whichever he finds more rewarding.

By going through this cycle of retraining again and again, factoring ever greater inhibition into the dog's mind towards lunge-nipping, fulsomely rewarding him for not lunge-nipping at things he might have lunge-nipped at before, and teaching him ever better impulse control, you really can turn this kind of behaviour around in Collies. I have been through this retraining process with so many dogs over the years.

Also be aware that many Collies can have lunge-nip reactions towards things like traffic, or household objects, but will not show aggression in other contexts. Thus, the lunge-nip impulse in a Collie, in itself, doesn't necessarily make him an aggressive dog.

Aggression towards other people or dogs

Aggression in Collies towards other – and typically less familiar – people or dogs is, alas, not that uncommon. It is primarily motivated by factors like fear of the new, poorer social awareness and impulse control, a greater need for control in general, plus any more learned extra elements from this behaviour that the dog has acquired in life. This could include how effective or rewarding aggression has been for the dog, as a strategy, in the past.

If you own, or have ever owned, a Collie with this kind of social problem you will be aware of how stressful it can be. Others may imply it is your fault, even though you can't think of anything you have done differently with the rearing or socialisation of your dog, compared to other people whose Collies are not aggressive.

Undeniably more skilful early rearing and social conditioning of any Collie (as outlined in Book Two of this series) is going to make a sizeable difference to the way he later turns out, in terms of his wider social tolerance towards others. But at the same time, a lot of social aggression problems in Collies still tend to have a high genetic factor involved. If you have a brain that not only predisposes you towards some more specific social fears, but also opts for a more defensive reaction to them, then it is clearly going to be that much harder for you not to be aggressive.

Social avoidance

When you have a dog who is aggressive towards other dogs or people he knows less well, it can understandably cause you some considerable stress and anxiety. And as with fear avoidance in the last chapter – where owners opt to actively avoid experiences that inspire less pleasant fear reactions in their dogs – the same can apply with aggression. Owners may think the best answer to a socially less tolerant and more aggressive Collie is to keep avoiding social situations that trigger his aggressive behaviour, rather than striving to teach him ever better social tolerance, so that aggression becomes a less necessary impulse in him.

The end result of such persistent social avoidance can be some pretty lonely walks out with your dog, or far fewer trips out with your dog, period, and only to places or contexts that he will tolerate. There will also be a notable downturn in the number of people visiting your home. And thus, bit by bit, your Collie has sucked you into his own social problems and hang ups, and made them heavily impact on your own life quality, too. This is a scenario I have seen time and time again.

Also, the smaller a Collie's social world becomes, the worse his fear and aggression often becomes whenever pushed to move much beyond it.

Breaking the social fear and aggression cycle

Owners often fail to realise how much of their Collie's aggression towards other dogs or people, when out, is inspired purely by fear. That is until I ask them to give their dog to me for a moment, on the lead, while they go some distance away or sit in their car.

As soon as they do this, more often than not, the seemingly 'ferocious' dog that was seconds ago lunging, snapping and snarling at every passing dog, is transformed. Other dogs and people continue to pass by without him even appearing to notice them, let alone react to them, as his only thought now is trying to get back to the safety of his owner and car.

Owners who witness this often feel bad. For they imagine that they must have somehow been instrumental in 'enabling' their dog's aggression in the past, or that in some way it must have been their fault.

But actually what happens is this. In order to react aggressively to passing dogs and people, the dog has to connect a very specific social 'picture' or context in his head with a particular impulse and reaction (i.e. aggression) he has carried out many times before. And this picture must include his owners.

If you remove the owners from this social picture, it is no longer the same. The dog's mind immediately recognises this and is thrown into greater doubt and confusion, as well as a loss of confidence when it comes to repeating his previous aggressive behaviour when other dogs or people pass. This doubt, confusion and loss of earlier confidence is then quickly replaced by the anxiety he feels about being separated from his owner. This anxiety, in turn, outweighs any other consideration in the dog's head – including passing dogs or people – other than to get back to his owner again.

This is just another fascinating example of how a dog's sub-conscious mind – all it feels and all it has learned – drives his behaviour. It is also a reason why separating owners initially from their socially aggressive dogs, is often the first step to their rehabilitation, and the development of different and healthier social pictures in their dogs' minds, which in turn invite better reactions.

Building new social associations

If you are out on a walk and you see two paths immediately ahead of you, one that seems a bit less certain or untrodden, and the other far more firmly worn and established, your instinct is usually to go for the latter. And the mind can work in exactly the same way, in preferring to stick to what is most familiar and ingrained.

So think of this parallel when it comes to reworking the attitudes of dogs with social

aggression issues. Their first instinct, when more socially challenged, will always be to do what they did in the past – i.e. react aggressively – because it feels most natural and familiar to them. Not reacting aggressively, on the other hand, is far less charted territory for them, mentally. So they are going to need considerably more in the way of incentives to not only try this path, but also to choose it more often in the future. They may also need to find the more ingrained mental path – i.e. aggression – a lot less rewarding in the future.

Dogs – and the pressures of poorer social awareness

You may have witnessed, or been in, situations where a dog has suddenly attacked another dog, or person, and you cannot for the life of you understand why. The dog, or person who got attacked, looked "perfectly friendly" or completely unthreatening to you, and thus did nothing seemingly obvious to invite such an aggressive response.

But this is because you possess a far higher level of social judgement and awareness; namely, an ability to better distinguish between more benign or threatening social signals, or intentions, in others. It is an ability we so take for granted that it never occurs to us what it might be like not to possess it, as can be the case with many autistic people, and also a lot of dogs, including Border Collies.

For dogs of this type, all social encounters or experiences take on a far higher degree of mental pressure and anxiety as they struggle to match what they are seeing in front of them with the right physical response, i.e. more positive or negative. Or they might initially start off with a more positive social response, and then suddenly their mind decides no, that was wrong! Now they should respond more aggressively instead. Such social reactions can happen or change in fractions of seconds, due to the mind's greater confusion. This helps explain so many otherwise seemingly less explicable, or predictable, patterns of aggression in dogs. You simply could not see or feel what they did in that moment when they attacked.

Often poorer social awareness can be evident in dogs who are only months old. There is no

THE HEAT OF THE MOMENT

Instinctive defence responses in Collies, resulting from poorer social awareness and impulse control

This picture sequence features an example of how poorer social awareness and impulse control in a Collie can result in defensive aggression (or a classic breed 'lunge-nip' reflex) towards others, including owners.

Social 'blind spots' and confusion:
In this first picture, the dog has insufficient time (or social awareness) to realise that the object rapidly approaching her at eye-level is her owner's hand, which, in turn, triggers a more instinctive defensive-aggressive reaction towards it.

Hang on, I know you:
In this second picture, the dog recovers and has a more conscious recognition that the approaching hand and her owner are connected. As a result, she abandons her previous more instinctive defence response and switches to more affectionate or appeasing behaviour.

Owners may often see the switch from aggressive to appeasing behaviour – as illustrated above –as the dog feeling 'sorry' or 'bad' about what he has just done. However, due to previously mentioned issues of poorer social awareness and impulse control, the dog may really struggle to stop himself reacting more defensively towards anyone, or anything, once a threat signal has reached his brain. Dogs like these require far more work, in general, on their levels of impulse control and also their social tolerance towards others approaching them more suddenly or closely..

PHOTOS: CAROL PRICE

relaxed tolerance, or obvious 'give and take' in their social interactions with others, or any clear recognition that a specific social signal or overture, from another person or dog, requires a suitably appropriate social response in return. They may prefer to hide from, or evade, all newer social interactions because they find them so worrying and confusing. Or they may try to neutralise the fear or anxiety such interactions produce by taking control of them in a more forceful or aggressive way. For example, by trying to 'body slam' other dogs, herd them, or put their heads over their necks. Or just lunge out and snap at both dogs and people.

Poor social awareness does not always result in aggression in dogs, but in dogs who have a stronger instinct to react to mental pressure with aggression, it is often a major exacerbating factor. It can also be a major factor in dogs who attack their owners or other family members (see *aggression towards owners and other household members, page 103*).

In Book Two of this series I highlighted how vital it is to give Collies a kind of social training and conditioning that bypasses their need to make more appropriate social judgements for themselves. It is from the confusion they feel about making these judgements that anxiety so often arises, and thereafter their more negative physical responses.

The social training in question includes the teaching of more set, if not ritualistic, patterns of behaviour when meeting other people or dogs. Thus taking a lot of the pressure of otherwise poorer social awareness or judgement away.

Stretching social tolerance

When trying to progressively stretch the social tolerance of dogs, and lower their need to feel aggressive towards others, I usually begin with people and dogs (including my own) who not only have greater experience of dogs with their kinds of problem, but whom I can implicitly trust. For one of the greatest obstacles to curing dogs of their social fear and aggression issues can be other dogs or people you meet, when out, who simply heap greater pressure on them, via their more intrusive or less considerate behaviour.

Dogs with social fear issues do not like being directly approached or engaged with, or feeling 'crowded in' in any way. Especially by those they know less well, including people who think they are "brilliant with dogs". Dogs who are fearful of social situations like distance, and respect for their space, while they begin the process of adjusting their previous mental outlooks and behaviours. Moreover, often it is simply the fear of a more overly intrusive approach, from another dog or person, that triggers an aggressive impulse in more socially anxious dogs, from further and further away.

Ultimately I work on exposing dogs to more and more dogs and people (or whatever their main issue is) at a level they can tolerate without the aggression impulse being fired, while also constantly rewarding them for more tolerant or confident behaviour. If I think a dog has got a far too active aggression impulse, which stands in the way of him learning better social attitudes, I may also need to use a deterrent to address this, in the form of a spray collar. Sometimes dogs do not need a spray collar deterrent, in order to rework their social attitudes and responses, just more constant benign social exposure and rewards. But at other times they need both.

As with fear issues, it can often involve lengthy and painstaking work to turn troubled dogs around in this way, to the point where they no longer feel the same need to behave aggressively towards others. You have to work in a series of small progressive steps to make any change in behaviour long lasting. But when you see the difference such changes can make to the lives of both dogs, and their owners, it is always, always worth it.

The value of one to one training – and role models

It is my belief that dogs with social aggression issues invariably benefit most from an individual, one to one, training approach, with the use of more experienced helpers – human or canine.

My view is also that dogs, just like people, often need better role models to observe and learn from, in their journey to developing better social behaviours. And time and time again, I have seen socially anxious/aggressive dogs learn so much

FOOD GUARDING AGGRESSION – AND WHAT TO DO ABOUT IT

Collies with greater control issues and impulses can sometimes become aggressive around their food bowls. This can be a problem that rapidly escalates if you do not handle it in the right way, to the point where you cannot even be in the same room with your dog while he eats, without him reacting aggressively. Also be aware that this is a purely instinctive impulse and reaction in your dog, rather than behaviour directed more personally at you.

To tackle this problem do the following.

1. First remove your dog's food bowl. His food bowl – and whole area around the food bowl, where he usually eats – provides an established 'guarding zone' for him, which can then more progressively widen out.

2. Once you have removed the food bowl, then set aside your dog's daily food allowance in a container. You will be feeding him this by hand for the foreseeable future, and always in return for him doing something for you.

3. Starting off in a room or place that is different to where he usually eats (i.e. not the kitchen, if that is where you have fed him previously) begin by getting your dog to 'sit' and 'watch you'. Or lie 'down' and 'watch' you. Or 'recall' and 'watch' you. (All training covered in Book Two).

4. Every time your dog cooperates, praise him and reward him with a piece of food from his daily allowance. In the future, your dog must cooperate with you in this way, in order to get his entire daily food allowance, piece by piece.

5. This way you have not only removed the former 'guarding zone' your dog had, round his bowl, and the impulses attached to it, you can also improve your dog's training and further ingrain habits of focus and cooperation in your dog.

6. If you ever want to go back to the habit of feeding your dog in a bowl, do so very gradually. Begin by placing the bowl in a different place to where it was originally located. Get your dog to do something for you, as before, e.g. 'sit' and 'watch'. Then place a piece of food in the bowl for him to eat. Repeat the process for every bit of food you put in his bowl.

7. If your dog continues to show no aggression, progress to getting your dog to do something for you, then putting a handful of food in his bowl, and moving this around with your hands, before allowing him to eat it. If he still shows no aggression, repeat this exercise.

8. You want your dog to learn that when you are around his food bowl, it can only be a positive thing as it is how he gets his food. And only when his sub-conscious mind reliably ingrains this lesson – and thereafter switches off more defensive impulses previously linked to a sense of threat – will he stop being aggressive around his food bowl.

9. If you ever have reservations about your dog's behaviour around his food bowl becoming aggressive again, always err on the side of caution and stick to the original tactic of only ever feeding him by hand. Additionally, as with all aggression problems, make sure you have suitable professional help, and supervision, from a behaviourist throughout this retraining.

Keep away from my stuff! Aggressive defence of most prized resources, like food, can be one of the most primal impulses in dogs. The same impulse can also be activated to maintain control over personal space, or territory, or even a most favoured owner. People may often read the latter as 'protective' or 'jealous' behaviour on their Collie's part, without realising that owners, too, can be regarded as one of the dog's most valuable life resources.

PHOTO: CAROL PRICE

from my own socially well-adjusted dogs, whose company gives them not only greater confidence, and reassurance, but also such clearer behavioural rules or codes to copy in life. This is a vital extra consideration for dogs whose levels of social awareness or recognition might otherwise be poor.

There will always be things that only dogs can teach other dogs, and the value of canine mentors, or role models, in any troubled dog's life, should never be underestimated.

For all these reasons I find it harder to see the merits of placing dogs with social aggression issues in one big class together, where they all feed off each other's flashpoints, insecurities or neuroses. Nobody in any school would put all the worst kids together in one class, and expect it to have any positive effect on their later behaviour. In fact usually it is quite the reverse.

Aggression towards visitors to the home

Some owners may find that their Collies develop aggression issues towards visitors to the home and, most particularly, towards those who are less familiar. Though do appreciate that dogs with poorer social awareness might not always easily recognise people they have met before, even many times, when they come to the home.

Either way, typically the more fearful dog may either choose to first go and hide somewhere, away from the visitor, then only become aggressive – i.e. growl, bare his teeth, snap or bark – when more active pressure is put on him, by owners, to meet or greet the visitor. Or the visitor, unintentionally, applies this extra pressure on the dog, via a more sudden intrusion into his space to "say hello".

Alternatively the dog may try to launch a more offensive attack of some kind on the visitor, in an attempt to keep him or her out of his space or home territory. Dogs who bark more aggressively at visitors in a constant action of moving forward, then backwards, as they do so, paint a classic picture of a dog in a state of greater social panic and confusion as to what he should do – i.e. attack or retreat from the 'fear object' ahead. This is often as a result of the previously mentioned poorer social awareness, or just insufficient social training and experience.

Better social training

In Book Two of this series, I highlighted how dogs could be trained to find household visitors far less worrying, with the teaching of the 'go see!' command, and also by owners taking greater charge of both the front door area, and their dog's whole behaviour, whenever visitors came. This is as opposed to imagining that their dog could just work out, all by himself, why these stranger people were in his home, and what he should do about it.

Often problems with visitors get worse as a result of this confusion on the dog's part, as well as the greater pressure that has been placed on the dog to actively greet a stranger when he did not want to, preferring to stay under a table or other place where he felt safer instead. So if your dog's first instinct is to run and hide from visitors, leave him where he wants to hide and do not pressurise him any further. Then start work on the kind of social training – including the 'go-see!' command – highlighted in Book Two of this series (Chapter 9), to progressively build up his social confidence.

More controlling reactions

Sometimes Collies will exhibit the anxiety, or insecurity, they feel about stranger visitors to the home in more controlling ways. A typical example being a dog who goes to sit right next to a visitor, in order to better observe and control their movements. If the visitor moves more suddenly towards him, he may growl. Or if the visitor goes to stand up, he may growl and look more threatening. Or the visitor might stroke the dog and then, as soon as they stop doing this, the dog growls or becomes aggressive.

I view this as a potentially far more dangerous reaction, motivated more by a need to control than classic fear. It can also be a behaviour consistent with the generally more dangerous canine mind model outlined earlier in this chapter. If you add to this reality the fact that you are leaving both the dog – and your visitor – at the mercy of his own more instinctive judgements and impulses, from moment to moment, it is all just too risky – especially if your dog has shown aggression towards visitors before. You do not want to give your dog any more opportunities to keep repeating and reinforcing

Control obsessions: A deeper rooted urge, and need, to protect personal territory and resources can spark more aggressive reactions in some Collies.

aggressive behaviour with visitors.

Once dogs have shown this level of controlling and aggressive behaviour towards visitors, this is one of the rare instances where avoidance of the aggression trigger is the most favoured future option. The dog should not be allowed freer or more repeated access to visitors again. It might not seem the most ideal solution, but it is always harder to retrain dogs whose aggression is essentially less predictable or logical in origin, and driven by deeper impulses you will never be able to reliably anticipate or understand. And the highest priority of all is to keep your visitors safe.

Dealing with space and territory related aggression

Some Collies can develop highly reactive and defensive patterns of aggression towards others who suddenly invade their space, or appear to threaten their more prized resources, including in the home. In essence this is 'survival' thinking and reacting at its most primitive level, but knowing that does not make it any easier to live with.

Typically the dog may lunge and snarl or snap but not bite. Once you have identified this kind of behaviour in your dog, there is a lot you must start doing differently, with regards to minimising his aggressive reactions over space and territory within the home environment. First, what parts or elements of territory is he most keen to take possession of, and then guard defensively from others? Is it the top of the stairs, the hallway, the front door area, or even a particular chair or sofa? Next, once you have identified them, simply do not allow him access to these places or things. Dogs cannot guard what they cannot have access to. It is better your dog has limited quarters at home, than ample opportunity to react aggressively to people and then – even worse – find this rewarding in some way.

It is also helpful to keep a long line on your dog at all times at home. You can then slowly and gently pick this up at the end, and move your dog calmly to wherever you want him to go, without forcing an aggressive confrontation, as can happen when more reactive dogs are suddenly approached and/or grabbed by their collars.

Sometimes these measures are all you need to stop, or prevent, defensive behaviours in your Collie revolving around space or territory. However, sometimes Collies can move on to dangerous patterns of aggression toward owners or other household members.

Aggression towards owners and other household members

When Collies show aggression towards their owners, or other household members, it may simply involve more acute defense instincts, less appropriately fired (just covered in *Dealing with space and territory related aggression*). But it can also revolve around a more obsessive need for control, plus often readier threat perception, poorer social awareness, and poorer impulse control. When all these factors combine, they can result in a dog with a potentially incendiary and dangerous mind.

Depending on the strength or readiness of aggression used, I always see Collies biting owners or other household members as the crossing of a red line. The genie – in terms of the dog's loss, or total absence, of any inhibition about attacking family members – is out of the bottle, and is not likely to go back in. For once a dog discovers the power of his aggression to control others he lives with, it is not a lesson he is likely to unlearn, or not want to repeat. And we are talking about a very primitive, but nonetheless often highly compelling, form of dog behaviour.

Sometimes owners try to fight fire with fire, by physically punishing dogs for showing this serious kind of aggression towards them, not realising how little control the dog often has over his own impulses, including how he behaves towards them. Moreover such punishments invariably ramp up the sense of threat owners represent in the dog's mind, making future aggression towards them even more likely.

There can be occasions when controlling aggression of this kind in a dog, towards owners or family members, is being fuelled or greatly exacerbated by some extra source of stress in his life. This could be physical pain, a major domestic upheaval that has shattered his whole sense of security, or some other continuing anxiety. And once the source of stress or anxiety has been resolved, the more controlling aggression that went with it goes as well.

At other times, however, it is just part and parcel of the dog's whole instinctive way of thinking and reacting to his surrounding world. Whereupon the prognosis is somewhat bleaker. I am continually amazed at the forbearance of some owners with Collies like these, prepared to go on living with a dog who could attack them at any time, and I also fully understand why people get to the point when they cannot live with it anymore.

Dogs who are most dangerous often tend to be most autistic in their thinking and behaviour, with more extreme aggression being just one of a wider range of mental problems or struggles they may have with life. Once you know that a dog has a more autistic mind, you might then have lower expectations of his behaviour than you did before you knew this. But it still does not make that behaviour any easier to live with.

I think that one of the cruellest things you can do to any owner is to give them false hope, and allow them to imagine that an aggression issue that stems chiefly from their dog's whole mental wiring can be magically cured. It is crueller still to ever let them believe that their failings as owners, alone, are what cause their dog to be the problem he is, as opposed to a far more complex and intractable range of mental issues.

An end to shaming and blaming

Hopefully this chapter will have given you a better insight into why different types of aggression occur in Collies, the typical motivations behind them and the extent to which they can be better addressed or handled in individual dogs. And also when they may be less amenable to a cure.

Mostly what I would like readers to take away from this is the realisation of how much aggression in dogs begins with the way they are mentally wired, and not just the way they are owned. It is a truth that is not always sufficiently told and still, in our wider canine culture, owners too often experience shame and blame for problems in dogs that are more rooted in their deeper genetic design. It is not helpful to the owners, or helpful to the dogs in question.

In forever blaming owners, moreover, we are also straying ever further away from a far bigger picture and question. Which is what is it about the way we breed dogs today that keeps producing the same recurring problems with their psychological health and behaviour.

CHAPTER 10:

SENSORY DETOX

Mental and sensory over-arousal in the Border Collie;
How to own a dog with a calmer and 'cooler' mind

The key to optimum physical and psychological health in your Collie is keeping him in
sufficient mental balance.
PHOTO: CAROL PRICE

Throughout this series, I have repeatedly emphasised how excess mental arousal is often the enemy of better or calmer behaviour in a Border Collie. As well as the exacerbating factor in many less desirable breed reactions, including aggression, and more manic and 'hyper' behaviour patterns, like spinning, circling, barking and just more crazily running around.

In Book One I explained the need to imagine that your dog's mind contains a mental thermometer, and the higher the temperature goes – in terms of levels of mental arousal – the higher his levels of reactivity will become. At the same time his levels of impulse control will decline. Thus, there will always be a direct correlation between the temperature of your dog's inner mental thermometer, and the nature of his external physical behaviour.

In Book One I also explained the whole biology of stress in dogs, and how the hormonal and physiological reactions brought about by mental arousal can affect a dog physically and psychologically, both shorter or longer term.

Shorter and longer term stress effects

The healthiest kind of stress system, and response, is one where periods of mental arousal are only infrequent and short lived in a dog, then immediately displaced by some kind of physical reaction or activity to burn up the adrenaline effects produced. Whereupon the dog returns to mental and physical balance again, as commonly happens with working dogs. The working Collie's natural mental pattern, in other words, is to combine longer periods of sustained concentration and balance with shorter periods of higher arousal and greater physical exertion. This kind of stress response is also most ideal for people.

However, the problem we have today, in people as well as dogs, is that while our inner stress systems and responses, in evolutionary terms, remain pretty antique in nature and function, our modern world brings an unremitting series of new challenges for them to deal with. This includes everything from greater environmental noise and crowding, to work and social pressures, plus sitting, fuming, in a traffic jam. This more sustained drip, drip, drip of different sensory and psychological challenges to

deal with means the brain and body get less and less respite from stress and, thus, less and less time to recover from its effects and regain a healthier state of balance.

Stress and the Border Collie

Now if you imagine how stressful modern life – on a sensory, social and psychological level – can be for us, just imagine how much more magnified the effects can become on the brain of a Border Collie, with its higher sensory sensitivity and lower ability to filter what it absorbs from its external surroundings, in the way of sound, light or movement. Add to this the kind of social pressures these dogs may face in more crowded or over-stimulating human environments every day, and you begin to understand why more persistent states of stress can be so common in the breed.

Symptoms of more persistent arousal – and stimulation addiction

I have known many Collies in this kind of more persistently stressed state, as well as owners who get so used to the picture of their dog in a chronically stressed state that they come to think that this hyper version of him is his more 'normal' personality – when it is not. It is a dog, instead, whose mental thermostat is stuck at the wrong end of the temperature scale.

Another problem that can arise in Collies that are perpetually over-aroused in this way is that they can then rapidly progress to becoming stimulation addicts. In other words, the dog becomes progressively more addicted to the state of being mentally aroused. He will then more actively look for new sources or triggers of mental arousal, all the time, on top of any occurring more naturally in his environment. This is a cycle of behaviour that, once started, can take some while to wind down again.

Self-stimulatory behaviour like this in autistic people is known as 'stimming'. It is also thought to have its roots in stress of some kind.

The cooling down process

In order to begin the process of cooling down your dog mentally, if you think he is persistently stressed, or over aroused, it can help to have a

Adrenalin junkies: Collies do not always have a healthier 'off' switch, and thus may excessively over arouse themselves with activities like chase games, unless you better control them.

better picture in your head of what a Collie should be, or look like, when not in a more persistent state of stress. If only to have some more tangible model of behaviour and mental outlook to aspire to, in your own dog.

Typically this is how I would define, or recognise, the more mentally balanced Collie:

- He has optimum concentration and responsiveness to commands or requests, instead of appearing mentally distracted, or unreachable, a lot of the time.
- He isn't constantly fidgeting around and whining, or forever looking for new sources of mental stimulation in his environment to react to.
- He can sit or lie still quite happily for prolonged spells of time, when asked, or after activity.
- He has no difficulty whatsoever going to sleep and staying asleep.
- He doesn't mount more extreme physical reactions to every new source of sound or movement around him.

This is what it means for your dog's mind to be in better balance.

Also be aware that higher stress-loads can often result in *physical* problems in Collies, too, such as digestive or skin problems, or the dog perpetually chewing or licking himself. So watch out for these signs.

The struggle for balance
Some Collies may have greater difficulty maintaining, or regaining, mental balance, not just because they are exposed to more stress but also because they have more reactive and impulsive minds, and weaker calming mechanisms. We can often forget that dogs have mental and hormonal systems for 'calming down', as much as they do for 'winding up' and in some the former may not be as efficient as the latter. So it is something worth factoring into the whole stress equation in your own dog.

Having looked at the way in which more persistent stress may affect Collies, I am now going to move on to a special 'sensory detox' programme designed for dogs whose minds require greater cooling down.

Sensory detox: winding down from excess adrenaline arousal and addiction

Sensory detox is a programme I advise putting Collies through in order to define how much of their heightened stress is down to sensory stimulation/over-arousal within their immediate environment. This includes any additional – though usually inadvertent – pressure placed on the dog by an owner's different approaches or interactions with him, or those initiated by other household members.

Other issues such as diet, and where you place your dog's rest quarters, are also considered.

This programme is particularly useful for dogs who display more on-going or extreme physical/behavioural symptoms related to persistent arousal.

The sensory detox programme is best carried out initially for two days; a weekend, for instance, would be ideal. If you see any real benefits in your dog's mental state at the end of two days, you may want to continue the programme for longer. It can also be a good programme to use in the early rehabilitation of rescue dogs, who may often arrive with high pre-existing stress loads.

WHICH DOGS CAN BENEFIT MOST FROM SENSORY DETOX?

Collies who can benefit most from the sensory detox programme are those who may be continually displaying these kinds of symptoms:

- Being chronically restless and agitated and finding it hard to settle down or sleep.
- Being particularly reactive to sound, movement or any other form of external stimulation.

When more abnormal seems normal: Owners can get so used to seeing their Collies in a more 'hyped up' mental state that they come to imagine this is normal for the breed — when it is not.

PHOTO: CAROL PRICE

- Whining, panting or fidgeting persistently, or scratching and biting themselves obsessively (especially, in the latter case, if other possible causes for this, such as parasites or allergies, have been ruled out).
- Obsessively seeking, or needing, attention from others.
- Indulging in persistent habits such as paw licking or tail chasing or spinning or chewing household fittings or furniture, or bedding and toys, and sometimes even swallowing bits of these.
- Continually looking for physical activities – for example digging, barking, eyeing and chasing things – to displace their stress, or to keep their adrenaline levels sustained.
- Showing more reactive/defensive aggression responses towards others. This is because adrenaline always heightens an animal's defence mechanisms.
- Displaying fairly low powers of concentration, or ability to absorb and respond to anything you say.
- Some highly stressed dogs may also show a distinct redness or glazed appearance in the eyes.
- Chronically stressed dogs may also have a poorer appetite and body condition.

Preparations

Before day 1 of sensory detox, first make the following preparations:

- Establish the best place in the house for your dog's rest or 'wind down' quarters. It should be somewhere where he will not only be exposed to the least possible amount of noise and movement, but also light. Thus somewhere with lower light levels, but not complete darkness. Remember that dogs have far better vision in lower light conditions than we do and, similarly, greater sensitivity to brighter light.

- An indoor kennel – covered with a blanket on the top and three surrounding sides – is ideal as a rest place, as you may sometimes need to shut your dog here for a while in order to help him better wind down. (*See The purpose of the enforced rest area*). Put some really comfy bedding inside it as well, unless he begins trashing this to better stimulate himself when you want him to rest. Do not leave any toys in there for the same reason.

- Your dog's rest area should also be well away from places like the front door, or front windows, where he may remain continually alert and reactive to anyone coming in or passing by.

- Prepare your dog's daily food allowance in advance. You will not be feeding this in a bowl. You will be encouraging him to find it for himself (*as outlined in a moment*), or earn it through more preferable behaviours. So set aside half of his daily food allowance for rewarding preferable behaviours, and the other half for your dog to find for himself.

- Ensure that your dog's food contains nothing in the way of artificial additives, colourings or preservatives, any of which could have a more stimulating effect on his mind.

- Attach a lead to your dog's collar and leave it there. Do not put a good lead on if you think he may bite or chew it. Alternatively use a length of rope or nylon washing line, around one metre (3 ft) long, and tie this to his collar. If you have any jobs round the home that require you to use louder tools or machinery, do these before the sensory detox period begins, and not once it is in progress.

THE PURPOSE OF THE ENFORCED REST AREA

During sensory detox you will need a special rest area where you will put your dog each and every time he shows symptoms of greater excitability, agitation or stress.

Apart from being an environment of far lower sensory stimulation, the reason you may need to have the option of shutting him away is because he may not otherwise stay there of his own accord. This would mean you could not effectively control his exposure to further sensory stimulation and arousal.

Dogs who are less used to being placed in confined spaces, or find the experience worrying, or are most stressed/aroused in general, may have a more extreme and longer-lasting distress or protest reaction when you first start sensory detox (i.e. barking, whining, howling, pacing restlessly around). And you should be prepared for this. Your dog is basically coming 'cold turkey' out of his stimulation/adrenaline addiction, and it won't be easy for him at first – or you. However, if you do not ride out these early withdrawal symptoms, he will never be able to learn how to get calmer again, or train his mind and body to do this more consistently or effectively.

Only ever use the enforced rest area when your dog is entering, or has entered, a more over-aroused and excitable mental state, or is displaying more generally agitated or restless behaviour. Whenever he is calmer, remove him from this area and let him have his freedom again, which is just another reward for calmer behaviour.

Communication without words: Appreciate the benefits of regularly interacting with your dog without speech or more intrusive physical handling. This will help to reduce human mental pressure in his life, and keep his stress levels as low as possible.

PHOTO: JUDI ASBURY

- Do not do any additional training with your dog of any kind during sensory detox, other than the exercises required for the programme.

Also be aware that putting your dog through sensory detox can sometimes be as challenging for you as it is for your dog, in terms of the greater self-discipline required on your part.

DAY 1

Your first priority on day 1 of sensory detox is to make your home as quiet as possible. Thus no loud music, or blaring televisions, or any other louder environmental noise that you may well have got used to, but which continues to cause brain pain for your dog. We can consistently underestimate how much stress is caused to Collies by the non-stop 'wall of noise' that exists in a typical domestic home.

On this day you will also use your dog's food allowance as rewards for the following actions:

- Coming to you or following you of his own accord, i.e. without being verbally asked by you.
- Going into his rest or 'wind down' place and maintaining a calmer or more wound down mental state.
- You will also need to set some food aside that he has to find for himself (*as outlined later*).

The next step is often the hardest for owners. And that is where – during the entire two days of sensory detox – *you do not touch your dog at all, or speak to him*. If you need to take or move your dog anywhere, do so by the lead or line you keep attached to him.

Initially it may be very strange not to talk to your dog at all, as for humans verbal expression is so automatic in our interactions with others. Plus, we have a tendency to really like the sound of our own voices. In fact, we are utterly addicted to the process of speaking to our dogs and can find it a very hard habit to break. However, communicating more via body language and signals than vocal expression comes far more naturally to dogs, and can often be far less stressful for them.

We may also not always understand how much of human speech and voice tone has some kind of pressure association attached to it for dogs. This could be because it has previously been connected to a negative or less desired approach from us – or someone else – or because dogs simply cannot understand what we are trying to communicate to them via speech.

They may also have stored many past memories of speech being attached to more hostile human body language, or actions, further intensifying negative connotations. Some dogs may become so desensitised to the constant noise and stress of human speech that they eventually switch off from listening to it altogether.

Why not talking makes a difference

Not talking to your dog may not only take some immediate pressure off him, it may also test how well you are able to communicate with him via body language alone, and without the additional weapon of verbal tone and pressure – i.e. come here, do this, do that – which we can tend to become heavily reliant on as a control device.

Another thing you may discover, through not being able to talk to your dog, is just how many interactions he may choose not to have with you, once you no longer verbally instruct him to do so. Thus, all in all, it can be a very revealing exercise.

If you wait for your dog to come to you when he wants to, as opposed to repeatedly impose yourself into his space, this can also take further pressure off him, by giving him a greater sense of control. This is a particularly important consideration for more confrontation sensitive dogs.

If you immediately lower your body position into a crouch, while at the same time turning sideways to your dog, and avert more direct eye contact with him – which is a far less confrontational and thus more inviting stance – he is more likely to approach you of his own accord. And every time he approaches you in this way, you can give him a bit of food from his daily allowance.

At the same time, if he doesn't want to come to you, don't force the issue. And just leave him be. Get

everyone in your household to follow the same non-talking and generally far less intrusive regime with your dog.

Reacting to the vacuum

Sometimes Collies become so addicted to constant sensory stimulation and arousal from their environment, and the adrenaline rushes that go with it, that the sudden deprivation of these stimulation sources, at the start of the detox programme, leaves them in a flatter mental vacuum that they are less able to tolerate. Much like a drug addict without their usual dose or fix.

So rather than immediately behaving in a quieter or more settled manner, when you remove some of these previous stimulants (i.e. noise, movement, light, talking, toys), your dog may try to recreate or sustain his more customary adrenaline levels in other ways. This could be rushing around barking at everything and anything, whining and fidgeting or digging holes, looking for things to eye and chase or push around. Any excuse to perpetuate the buzzed up state.

Some Collies may also actively seek to provoke more heightened physical or verbal reactions from you, which they can then use as further fuel to keep their adrenaline levels higher. A lot of owners may not understand that shouting or talking louder to a dog when he is in a more excitable state, or physically pushing or pulling him around in any way, always makes him worse, because it simply causes an additional stress response.

So be wise to this. It is important to see this mental/behavioural reaction for what it is; not a dog 'playing up' or more consciously deciding to be annoying, but one struggling to retain the kind of adrenalin levels he has long been used to. So do not stress or arouse your dog further with exasperated physical or verbal interventions on your part, which will only keep those levels higher.

Instead, keep very calm. As ever, do not say anything. Just take your dog gently by his lead to his rest/wind down area. Throw a bit of food in there for him, then leave him there until he settles down again. Keep doing this relentlessly, every time he acts in a more wound up way, only allowing him back out of this area when he has calmed down.

Toughing it out

Initially this may be a hard and testing process for all parties, as once some Collies have got into a very heightened state of mental arousal, and got very used to being in it, coming down from it can be a process not totally unlike an addict withdrawing from a drug.

Your dog may fidget, bark, whine, pant and pace around in his rest place, and do whatever else he can to keep his adrenaline levels higher. However, the fewer sources of mental/sensory stimulation that now exist in his resting environment, including any verbal input from you, the harder this will be for him. So you must try to tough it out.

Exercise

During day 1 of sensory detox, a lot of your time may be spent taking your dog back and forward to his rest space to calm down, until he gets better and better at this. And remember to keep rewarding your dog with food, whenever he shows calmer behaviour.

Your dog will also benefit from exercise, which can help to use up adrenaline. However, when you take him out, it must be a distance walk with minimum additional visual or sound stimulation. Go somewhere as quiet as possible, with less chance of meeting other dogs or people – and this is particularly relevant if your dog has issues with either, or both.

Also go somewhere where he is less likely to be exposed to crowds or traffic, particularly if he has issues with these. And strictly *no* toy chasing or other forms of chasing. As you are still not talking to your dog, you cannot verbally 'recall' him, and thus during the walk it is best to keep him on a longer lead or line.

Walking your dog for some distance without talking to him, touching or grabbing him, or throwing him his usual toy – which he may well be constantly expecting – may seem a really alien experience at first, which might take a little while for you both to get used to. However, it also gives his mind a far greater rest from stimulation.

Remember to keep rewarding your dog with food during the walk, every time he shows calmer or more relaxed behaviour, and every time he chooses to come to you of his own accord.

Food finding

You may recall that during preparation for the sensory detox programme you set aside half of your dog's food allowance for preferable behaviours, and the other half for him to find himself.

Finding food can reduce stress in dogs. First, because they need some level of concentration and focus to do it, and second because a dog finding his own resources can give him a greater sense of control.

Start by throwing a piece of food on the floor where your dog can see it and point to it – remember you are not talking to your dog. He should go and eat it. Then start putting food in different bits of the room, pointing to it each time. And do the same in the garden. Your dog should eventually learn that when you point, there is food around for him to find. You can decide where you want to hide food, and how difficult you want this hunt to be for your dog, in terms of how hard he has to work to find it. Though harder searches will keep your dog mentally occupied for longer.

Once dogs learn to find food in this way, they usually get better and better at it, even when you do not initially show them where you have hidden food, and just point – after you have hidden it – within a particular area instead.

Evening of day 1

By the evening of day 1 of sensory detox for your dog, it is likely that you will feel quite shattered – not just with constantly returning your dog to his rest place, whenever he shows more stressed or agitated behaviour, but with the additional strain of not being able to talk to him and doing so many other things differently.

And this is because changing old habits of behaving, in favour of new ones, can be just as testing for us as it can be for dogs. It is also the main reason why owners fail to improve their dog's behaviour, and remain stuck in their same old patterns of doing things with him.

So you may be feeling shattered after Day 1, and this is totally normal. But how is your dog? With any luck, he is going to be rather less stressed already and a lot more tired, too. And if you have done everything right, he should also have far less

Chilling time: The habit of winding down and resting, at set periods, should become just as regular a habit for your Collie as getting more wound up.
PHOTO: CAROL PRICE

difficulty going to sleep and staying asleep, which is a good sign of an already healthier mind.

DAY 2

On Day 2, repeat everything you did on Day 1. You may still find your dog gets agitated, and protests for some time when you then place him in his resting area to wind down again, because his mind is still a little in love with these old habits.

But what you might also find is that each time you put your dog in his resting place to wind down, it takes him less and less time to do so than it did the day before. This is a sure sign that his general arousal levels are falling. He may also have fewer and fewer episodes of frantic or agitated behaviour. And he may be more hungry.

On the evening of Day 2 you are finally going to talk to your dog again. Just say something simple, and speak quietly; use his name, for example. With his stress levels falling, his concentration returning, and the fact that you have not spoken to him in some while, he is far more likely to listen this time, and give you his full attention.

You are now well on the way to returning your dog to balance. Also be aware that the more quietly, and less often, you speak to dogs in general, the more likely it is that they will listen to you.

Post detox benefits

If sensory detox brings about some real benefits in your dog's mental state and behaviour, within just a couple of days, you now know what to do whenever he gets too aroused again. Or you may want to continue the programme for longer, if your dog has chronic over-arousal issues. Either way, the process should also have left you with some lasting lessons, in terms of the everyday stress we can inflict on dogs, without realising it. This is just through the way we handle or speak to them, or by allowing constant exposure to noisier and over-stimulating environments.

Some dogs will always be better at managing all this than others. But in my fairly lengthy experience, once you take excess stress and mental arousal out of the equation for a Border Collie – or at least significantly reduce it – you always end up with a rather different, and better, kind of dog.

What should also be remembered is how much our own mental states and moods can affect our dogs. Recently, a Swedish study revealed how the cortisol (or stress) levels found in humans are uncannily the same as those found in their dogs.

Use that brain

In general I would urge all Collie owners to consider the wider benefits of scentwork pursuits and tasks for their dogs, not only to enhance their concentration and better cool their minds, but also to make the most of their spectacular levels of sensory perception and brainpower. Most countries now have training organisations and classes that specialise particularly in scentwork, so just find out where your nearest one might be online, and get involved! To me, there is no finer sight in the world than a Collie totally in love with the power of his own brain, and what it can do.

Peace at last: Be aware that some Collies will always take longer than others to properly wind down, and regain mental balance. This is especially the case if they have been in a chronically aroused or stressed state for some time.
PHOTO: CAROL PRICE

CHAPTER 11:
LAST THOUGHTS
Border Collies past, present and future

So now we are coming to the end of a three-part book journey into the Border Collie, and everything that makes him unique as a dog. I hope this series has given you a far deeper insight into a breed that I have owned and admired for a greater part of my life, and which for so long has suffered from being misunderstood.

I also hope it inspires a wider awareness of the link that frequently exists between a certain kind of genetic mind in a dog, and the greater challenges he may face in life as a result, especially when destined to be a social companion.

For unless we are better aware of the mental differences, or disadvantages, some dogs may inherit, and why, we can never be in a position to better help or manage them, or find lasting solutions to their problems.

The past

Frequently, when trying to explain many of the behaviour or training issues I see in Border Collies today, or help their owners better understand and manage them, I think back to over a century ago, where this book series, and this breed, actually began.

I think about Adam Telfer and Old Hemp, in the late 1800s, striding across the remote reaches of the Northumberland countryside, moving livestock from one point to another. I think about how it must have been a place of such comparative stillness and quiet and peace, and where the only sensory and environmental challenges that existed for the dog were the bleating and movement of sheep, and the rush of the wind and the fall of the snow and the rain.

I think that Adam Telfer and his fellow breed founders created a dog, primarily, to fit this one kind of purpose, and one kind of world. And when he did, he could not possibly have looked into the future, and seen the different kind of purposes and different kinds of worlds into which Border Collies would later be plunged, despite having minds that remained pretty much the same as when they first evolved. The instincts, drives, compulsions and vulnerabilities, and the need to exert greater order and control over everything that approached or surrounded them in life remain unchanged.

But if he had been able to look into the future in this way, then I think he might also have predicted some of the challenges that could lie ahead for Collies as pets and social companions.

The present

As I write this book, the Border Collie is a dog, and breed, still continuing to evolve. There are now dogs at one end of the breeding spectrum – often, though by no means exclusively, show lines – with relatively low working character, drive or instinct. And then there are dogs bred for livestock or competitive pursuits with such high-octane working brains that they will inevitably bring more autistic characteristics with them.

It is not always realised how much skill and knowledge it takes for any breeder to consistently produce Collies who combine a good working brain with a highly sound – if not bombproof – social nature. But they are still, at least for me personally, the dogs I most prize and would always travel the extra mile to find.

The future

I do not know where Border Collies will be going in the future, or whether they may eventually diversify into a range of more distinctly different genetic types; i.e. the show Collie, sheep working Collie, agility Collie, obedience Collie and so on.

We may have dogs who look very different, and behave very differently, according to more specific genetic selection, and whether that proves to be a good thing for the breed as a whole, only time will tell.

Whatever the case, however, I still hope people never forget where all these dogs, as a breed and type, originally came from. As well as the instincts and attributes that will remain branded into their DNA for countless generations to come. For no dog ever truly escapes his earliest genetic origins. Border Collies are proud dogs, with an equally long and proud history, and that is something we should also never forget.

What I would also like to say is that whatever Collie we own, or prefer, the one thing that unites us all, worldwide, is a love for a breed that is truly remarkable and which, once known and owned, leaves its mark on us forever. A breed that, for over a century, has been intriguing us, baffling us, challenging us and astonishing us with its brilliance in equal measure. A breed whose origins began on the cold, barren, windswept and often forbidding hills of northern England, and rose to become the most intelligent, athletic and versatile dog on earth. It is a dog that is like no other, thinks and acts like no other, and one we are privileged to share our lives with.

Ultimately the Border Collie truly is a breed apart.

Preserving something special: The future of Border Collies, and how they continue to evolve as a breed, is down to all of us who love, respect and admire them, and consider them to be the most remarkable dogs on earth.

INDEX

A

Aggression in Border Collies 87-103

Aggression and a more dangerous canine mind model 89

Aggression and breeding 90-92

Aggression and the use of deterrents 94-96

Aggression motivators 90

Aggression prevention 90-92

Aggression resulting from poorer social awareness 98

Aggression towards other dogs and people 96-102

Aggression towards owners and household members 92, 103

Aggressive drive, more natural levels of, in individual dogs 26

Control aggression 28, 35, 44, 101-102

Deflected or displaced aggression 89

Fear aggression 73, 90, 96-97

Food and resource guarding aggression 100

Lunge-nip aggression 92-96

Territorial and space-sensitive aggression 24, 28, 37, 44, 88, 90-93, 101-102

Anxiety and anxiety related behaviours in Border Collies

Anxiety caused by change 36-37

Anxiety caused by potential loss of control 58, 72

Anxiety in very young puppies 92

Separation anxiety 30, 60-66

Social anxiety 24, 44, 90, 96-97

Arun, a dog with a heart of gold 3

Autistic aspects of the Border Collie 9, 11-12, 20, 22, 24, 25, 36, 39, 40, 41, 63, 72, 97, 103, 105, 115

Understanding more autistic patterns of behaviour in your dog 12

B

Behaviour differences and changes in Border Collies 15

Age-related behaviour changes in Border Collies 37

Changes related to adolescence, neutering or spaying 34-36

Changes related to medication, diet, pain or illness 33

Changes related to the stress of 'change' 36-37

Changes that occur more suddenly in your dog 32-37

Mental differences 59

Natural breed variation 15

The Collie Spectrum 16-31

Behaviour problems in Border Collies (see *Aggression, Anxiety and anxiety related behaviours, Chase behaviour, Controlling and manipulative behaviour, Fearful and phobic behaviours, Genetically related behaviour, Instinctive and impulsive behaviours, Obsessive and obsessive-compulsive activity, Self-stimulating behaviour, Sensory sensitivity and reactivity and Social problems and issues*)

Learning from failure 13

Motivation, impulse, physical reaction – the key mental behaviour sequence in dogs 76, 78, 82, 90

The key 'problem' traits 39

Understanding and changing the way your Collie thinks 14

When is your dog's behaviour a problem? 13

Why are some Collies more 'difficult' than others? 10-15

Why is your dog less responsive or 'obedient' than others? 48-59

Behaviourists and seeking help with your dog's behaviour 92, 95, 100

Beware of 'quick fixes' 19

Ben (Fear case study) 81

Border Collies past, present and future 114-117

C

Change intolerance and craving for 'sameness' in Border Collies 27, 30, 36, 42, 46, 63

More natural levels of change intolerance, in individual dogs 30

Chase behaviour in Border Collies 14, 17, 69, 73, 93, 110 (*Note: Anti-chase training is covered in Book Two of this series*)

Collie Spectrum, the

Assessing the nature of the dog you own 16-31

Control neuroses in Border Collies 44, 90, 93

Also available from First Stone Publishing

BORDER COLLIES: A BREED APART

Books One & Two

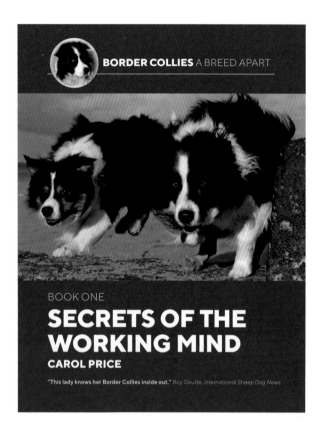

Secrets Of The Working Mind examines the breed's heritage; the legendary early dogs which shaped the Border's Collie's identity.

She explores working instinct and shows how the traits that go with it explain so many other aspects of the breed's psychology and behaviour.

Essential Life Skills & Learning focuses on the Collie learning process and what your dog's education should involve.

This includes teaching the essential life skills which Collies need if they are to face the world as happy, well-adjusted individuals.